PRIMERS

MW00778177

Narrative Architecture

PRIMERS

Narrative Architecture

NIGEL COATES

WILEY

A John Wiley and Sons, Ltd, Publication

This edition first published 2012
© 2012 John Wiley & Sons Ltd

Registered office

John Wiley & Sons Ltd, The Atrium, Southern Gate, Chichester, West Sussex, PO19 8SQ, United Kingdom

For details of our global editorial offices, for customer services and for information about how to apply for permission to reuse the copyright material in this book please see our website at www.wiley.com.

Executive Commissioning Editor: Helen Castle
Project Editor: Miriam Swift
Assistant Editor: Calver Lezama

ISBN 978-0-470-05745-2 (hardback)
ISBN 978-0-470-05744-5 (paperback)
ISBN 978-1-119-96320-2 (ebk)
ISBN 978-1-119-96306-6 (ebk)
ISBN 978-1-119-96307-3 (ebk)
ISBN 978-1-119-94348-8 (ebk)

Cover design, page design and layouts by Karen Willcox for aleatoria.com
Printed in Italy by Printer Trento Srl

Acknowledgements

Though limited in scale, this book has been a long time in the making. I first agreed to write it in 2006, the year in which Branson Coates Architecture evolved into Nigel Coates Studio. Far from weakening my argument, the passage of time has strengthened the thesis. It has allowed me to include many subsequent examples of narrative in practice and some of the most inventive projects done by students at the Royal College of Art while I was Professor of Architecture there. I am grateful to all the contributors of projects included, and to Howard Watson for his picture research in the early stages. I would like to extend my thanks to: Mark Garcia for his help in making an initial mapping of the subject; Helen Castle for her patience and detailed notes; and Will Hunter for his editorial overview and guidance in formulating the present structure. Thanks are due also to Amber Jeavons for delving into my studio archives, to Caroline Ellerby for her rigorous image management, and to Abigail Grater for overseeing the copy-editing stage. Lastly I would like to thank John Maybury, my partner in all creative ventures, and without whose tireless encouragement and literary lightness of touch, this modest work would not have come into being.

Picture credits

The author and the publisher gratefully acknowledge the people who gave their permission to reproduce material in this book. While every effort has been made to contact copyright holders for their permission to reprint material, the publishers would be grateful to hear from any copyright holder who is not acknowledged here and will undertake to rectify any errors or omissions in future editions.

l = left, r = right, t = top, b = bottom

Contents

Francesco Colonna, *Hypnerotomachia Poliphili*, Venice, Italy, 1499.

One of the first great achievements of print, this extraordinary Renaissance book combines text and woodcut to create a captivating vision. Struggling through the dark wood of medieval thought, its protagonist Poliphilo searches for his love but stumbles on mysterious temples and Dionysian rites.

Preface

The Author beginneth his Hypnerotomachia, to set downe the hower and time when in his sleepe it seemed to him that hee was in a quiet solitarie desart, and uninhabited plaine, and from thence afterward how he entered unadvisedly before he was aware, with great feare, into a darke obscure and unfrequented wood.

Francesco Colonna, *Hypnerotomachia Poliphili*, 1499[1]

Architecture is too big to hide. Even the ugliest buildings reveal something of the culture that made them, the faults there for all to see. Yet architecture is also a powerful instrument, a potent medium for democratic, religious or political power. From the humble house to the tallest tower, designers want their buildings to stand on tiptoes, to reach that bit higher than a response to utility. Desire is part of architecture's language; few would deny that every civilisation makes the most of its buildings. From the Incas of pre-Columbian America to the indigenous Ainu of Japan, from New York to New Delhi, from Dublin to Dubai, every culture looks to architecture for enduring messages, and to a certain articulation of life itself. Narrative provides a way of coming face to face with architecture in the 'dark and unfrequented wood' of the anything-goes culture of our times.

When civilisations clash, it is not just the people that suffer, but the infrastructure, the landscape and, of course, the buildings. Ancient Babylon was finally obliterated by the last Iraq war. In the wake of destruction, wars also make way for renewal. In the wake of the destruction of the Wall, Berlin was reshaped in a form that expresses German aspirations for a new society. Historically architecture may be divided into styles, but there are other less synchronised rhythms that mean that architecture is subject to a version of Darwin's theory of evolution. Going beyond manifestations of style, 19th-century Paris, with its broad avenues and galleries lined with boutiques, expresses the bourgeois need for observation and display. To understand the dynamics of architecture you need to fully surround yourself by its complex and often bewildering phenomena.

Whether in the service of power or vernacular commodity, architecture cannot avoid materialising the literature of cities. For every society, it always speaks a kind of lingua franca. Buildings have their own narratives: from the first impulse to build, to their realisation and prime, and to their decline. Like nature, architecture constantly dies and renews itself within the cultural ecosystem that makes up cities. So much can be read through buildings. As Edward Hollis says: 'Buildings long outlive the purposes for which they were built, the technologies by which they were constructed, and the aesthetics that determined their form; and soon enough their form and their function have little to do with one another.'[2]

Perhaps, in the early decades of the 20th century, people and populations were thrown into such turmoil that Modernist clean lines represented a way out of the embroiled hell they were living through. With the pluralism and the postmodern reflection that emerged in the closing decades of the last century, with the pull of embracing history, inevitably the many voices of a mixed society would be reflected in the way we build.

This book is partly an attempt to explore the potential for narrative as a way of interpreting buildings, but also signposts the way to architecture that is relevant to a multi-disciplinary and multi-everything age. Within this messy, complicated, multi-layered but ultimately exhilarating everyday world, it outlines what 'narrative architecture' is and its wider significance for designing and appreciating buildings.

In exploring narrative, I have no preordained theory from which a new architecture can spring. My approach summarises the intuitive response that some of us had when we formed the architecture group Narrative

Architecture Today (NATO) almost 30 years ago. Rather than diminishing, this first insight has turned into a steadily growing body of research that underscores the cultural rather than the scientific trajectory of architectural ideas. The term has since been absorbed into everyday culture, and is as common in news reports on subjects ranging from politics to sport. But in architecture I think it has a particular meaning beyond an overarching theme. It denotes a sensibility and a way of working that sets out to incorporate human nature into its method. In pursuit of meaning rather than performance, it frames an architecture that takes account of human experiences and the need to shape them into stories. It starts and ends with how people interact first and foremost with their environment, and in the process of responding to it and yielding to it, map their experiences in a mental space that architects need to understand, and possibly make use of.

Happy to hide behind archetypal forms like the pitched-roof shed/house/temple and the vertically thrusting tower/chimney/block, most architecture today deliberately avoids emotional engagement with its user. Alternatively narrative in architecture can fulfil not only a psychological need but a functional need as well. It is becoming a minimum requirement rather than an artistic and unnecessary add-on. Throughout a lifelong attachment to the discipline of architecture, I have been looking to break out of its closed-circuit audience to make it more relevant to the city dweller, understanding and developing strategies for bringing this into the process of design.

I begin this enquiry by looking at the evolution of narrative from what we now see as architectural history, and at the physical and psychological role of narrative in the cities we currently inhabit – as phenomenology. Narrative is a theme that is writ large in the social dynamics of our times; semiotic understanding of language, communication and identity has brought us virtually to the point where the language of architecture and those of advertising and the media cross over into one another's territories. Concepts of narrative are built into the post-millennial language of architectural debate, but relatively few of these concepts are organised in print. This book is not meant to be the last word on the subject, but more a primer that will encourage others to add to or contradict the interpretation of narrative that I have arrived at through my experience as a designer, academic and curious onlooker.

Each of the following chapters examines narrative in architecture from a particular vantage point. From beginning to end, the book loosely follows a chronological structure citing key events, designs and buildings. But within this, a taxonomy emerges. It is intended to help the reader make use of narrative as a methodology, one that is particularly suited to design in an age of communication.

References

1 Francesco Colonna,
Hypnerotomachia Poliphili,
Venice, 1499, first English
edition published in London,
1592.
2 Edward Hollis, *The Secret
Lives of Buildings: From the
Parthenon to the Vegas Strip
in Thirteen Stories*, Portobello
Books (London), 2009, p 9.

1

The Long Perspective

The terms 'narrative' and 'architecture' may not at first seem to be natural bedfellows. In today's sense they suffer from slightly oppositional problems: the former proliferated and diluted, the latter restricted and reduced. In the media, reference to 'narrative' is now so commonplace as to evade meaning. In its tightest form it indicates a literary sensibility, but often dissolves simply into an 'idea'. In the communication age, narration invades the everyday: 'What's happening?' is a question answered by every tweet on Twitter.

Much 20th-century architecture pursued an abstract aesthetic that married well with functional ideals. Modernism celebrated the fact that it had broken free from the 'tyranny' of decoration. And yet despite this, the built environment inevitably 'communicates' – it cannot avoid doing so. Like nature the city can speak primordially, its fabric tacitly conveying its rich and potent history. A financial centre – the City of London, or New York – expresses its economic power through its glossy tallness as much as derelict buildings disclose their story of decline.

And we have stories of our own; the curious citizen can easily discover architectural narrative everywhere. Narratives arise spontaneously in the course of navigating the world – from inside to outside, private to public, personal experience to collective myth. This reading of architecture doesn't require an architect to have 'written' it. Even unplanned settlements such as shantytowns or medieval villages contain complex narrative content; for an inhabitant they will configure a three-dimensional map of social relations, possible dangers and past events. Mental maps situate fragments in a time–

space continuum: a house where you once lived, or the scene of an accident. The city constitutes a rich theatre of memory that melds all the senses in ways that suit every single one of us, in our capacity to combine instinct and knowledge, rational understanding and the imagination.

Personal narratives build on the cognitive mechanisms that arise from existing places and spaces. Narrative has its roots in the world we inhabit, and occurs at the interface between our own experience and complex signs, like the little red pointers that smother other data on Google maps. It does not necessarily manifest as appearance; the fields in Flanders where so many First World War battles took place have an emotional significance as a site of loss but today look much like any other. We are walking encyclopaedias of architecture not because we've shaped it, but because we experience it.

This chapter asks how narrative applies to architecture. We shall see how narrative in space as opposed to literature or cinema has a firm basis in the way each of us learns to navigate and map the world around us. Within the framework of these personal spatial geometries, we will explore how narrative constructs can engage with the medium of space. This will provide a framework for how architecture can be invested with narrative as a means to give it meaning based on experience.

Narrative: from storytelling to spatial practice

Storytelling is as old as the hills. Even before the help of writing, universal myths were shaped by the oral tradition. From the Songlines of the Australian Aboriginals to the proto-myths of the Greeks, mankind has searched for answers to the mysteries of the universe, painting them on walls and encapsulating them in stories. Narratives enabled phenomena powered by the unseen forces of nature to be 'explained', and corralled into a system of beliefs. Their overarching themes lie at the heart of the major religions. Narratives that personify ethical or existential questions have profoundly shaped our understanding of space; these mythical tales and parables have the power to mediate between the spatial configuration of the universe, of heaven and hell, and the everyday world and its reality of survival, sustenance and territory. Within the framework of these spatial geometries, narratives can engage with the medium of space, and form the basis on which architecture can be given meaning.

With roots in the Latin verb 'narrare', a narrative organises events of a real or fictional nature into a sequence recounted by the 'narrator'. Along with exposition, argumentation and description, narration is one of four categories of rhetoric. The constructed format of a narrative can extend beyond speech to poetry, singing, writing, drama, cinema and games. Narration shapes and simplifies events into a sequence that can stimulate the imagination, and with its understanding comes the possibility of the story being retold – verbally, pictorially or spatially. Though they may involve shifts of time, location and circumstance as the dynamics of a plot unfold, for the viewer or the reader, stories progress along a sequential trajectory.

In architecture the linearity of the narrative function dissolves as the spatial dimension interferes with time. In architectural space coherent plot lines or prescribed experiential sequences are unusual. The narrative approach depends on a parallel code that adds depth to the basic architectural language. In a conventional narrative structure, events unfold in relation to a temporal metre, but in architecture the time element is always shifting in response to the immutability of the physical structure. While permanence should be celebrated as a particularly architectural quality, inevitably we should be curious about its opposite. The difference between a mere image and a work of art lies partly in its endurance – of existence but also of meaning. In architecture, that endurance is both positive and negative, depending on whether the public buys into it or not.

The various physical parts of a space signify as a result of the actions – and experiences – of the participant, who assembles them into a personal construct. The narrative coefficient resides in a system of triggers that signify poetically, above and in addition to functionality. Narrative means that the object contains some 'other' existence in parallel with its function. This object has been invested with a fictional plane of signification that renders it fugitive, mercurial and subject to interpretation. If a conventional narrative in a work of fiction binds characters, events and places within an overarching plot framework, in an environment narrative carries all of the above, but the fictional or self-constructed might be tested against physical reality. Narrative 'fictionalises' our surroundings in an accentuation of explicit 'reality'.

Like the system of trip wires and pressure-sensitive buttons hidden in the folds of a Baroque fountain, narrative in architecture is rarely a prescribed sequence of meanings, but is instead an anti-sequential 'framework' of associative meanings held in wait to 'drench' the unsuspecting visitor. In whatever form, it communicates subtly and unpredictably, and often works better when hidden rather than overt. In a physical environment, narrative construes what philosopher and novelist Umberto Eco (b 1932) calls a 'connotative' rather than a 'denotive' meaning that is close to function. The temple represents the god it houses rather than the denotive meaning of the act of worship.[1] In a world of postmodern, post-Structuralist understanding, the term 'narrative' has come to signify a level of meaning that substantiates the object, and yet contains an animated inner quality that interprets human events in relation to place.

The beginnings of architecture have been variously interpreted as the primitive hut,[2] or – according to Eco – the recognition that a cave can provide protection and shelter.[3] By the time the cave or the hut had fully formed as concepts, they must have featured as anecdotal homes. Myths and religions alike narrate the origin of the world in terms of everyday phenomena: in light and dark, in landscape and animals, and in men with supernatural powers. Since architecture can be manipulated and interpreted through narrative, it follows that the architect can invest architecture with a proportion of narrative alongside a response to the context and the programme of activities. Ancient temples of course tell stories, or highlights from them, as any visitor to the Louvre or the British Museum will appreciate.

Indeed, it is buildings that need the most potent symbolic content which make the most use of narrative strategies. Churches accumulate narrative as a result of the desire to reflect the story of God in every way possible, including the configuring of the body of Christ in their plan, their decoration, painting and sculpture. Northern Europe's great medieval cathedrals also tell complex stories of configuration, veneration and extremes of heaven and hell. With the help of the pointed arch, the multiple column and the flying buttress, every Gothic cathedral exhibits a rational organisation of the world through its geometry and, with its enormous soaring windows, the 'light of heaven'. Every aspect of these buildings has symbolic purpose, from the cruciform plan to details of capitals and windows.

Despite architecture usually being thought of as the art of articulating spaces, connotative meanings abound in its multi-various territories, and have done so from the outset. In architecture, narrative is a term that has risen in usage since the mid-1980s, but to grasp its implications, it would be valuable to visit some examples drawn from disconnected historical and physical contexts. What follows is distinctly not a history but a series of vignettes drawn from diverse times and places that together help define a context for narrative in architecture as an approach to practice. They are separated into the three gestalts; each one reveals narrative as the translation of a narrative spirit into a tangible, physical form.

Narrative awakenings

In the Palazzo Pubblico, the town hall of Siena in Italy, there is a frescoed state room that celebrates the relationship between the populus and

Ambrogio Lorenzetti, *The Allegory of Good Government*, Palazzo Pubblico, Siena, Italy, 1338–40.

One of three major frescoes that together make up the Sala dei Nove, this televisual composition uses the framework of Siena's collective architecture to weave daily events typical of a harmonious society.

its government, as had been expressed in the writings of contemporary chronicler Dino Compagni (c 1255–1324). The cycle of frescoes, *The Allegory and Effects of Good and Bad Government*, was painted by Ambrogio Lorenzetti (c 1290–1348) in the mid-14th century at a time when there was a need to stabilise civic ambitions. These two paintings representing good and bad face each other on opposite walls.

In the *Allegory of Good Government* everyday life is portrayed as a set of events occurring simultaneously. Unlike the extraordinary, usually religious occurrences represented in most painting of the period, this is an everyday scene with no apparent mishaps or strife. A narrative dimension builds on the commonplace. As opposed to blueprints of the architectural kind, in the painting the buildings constitute a backdrop, and in many ways their purpose was exactly that – a naturalistic *mise en scène* for the families that lived, and hopefully flourished, in and between them. On the opposite wall, the *Effects of Bad Government* includes decaying buildings, burning and a lot of cloak-and-dagger stuff. The painter's use of the whole room as a conceptual matrix reinforces this dialogue between good and bad. Although flattened by its blocked representational technique, the sense of space in these frescoes is palpable, with people in the foreground and buildings and towers in a very three-dimensional middle distance. Despite the absence of precise architectural representation, Lorenzetti employed a plausible vocabulary of building types. You can sense the narrow alleyways between the buildings, reinforcing what you might experience when walking back through the city. This room establishes a thoroughly accurate 'narrative' that has relevance today.

In mid-15th-century Florence, Giovanni Rucellai, head of a prominent wool merchant family, commissioned Leon Battista Alberti (1404–72), the leading exponent of the classical revival that came to be known as the Renaissance, to build a palace where, according to Rucellai's testimonial, 'out of eight houses, I made one'.[4] Alberti and his contemporaries were experimenting with building in the style of earlier, more poignant classical models. His design for the Palazzo Rucellai (1446–51) took its cue for the treatment of the orders of its pilasters from the Coliseum in Rome, with Tuscan capitals on the ground floor, Ionic on the first floor and Corinthian on the second. Rediscovered classicism was at the cutting edge of contemporary thinking to the extent of obsession and bitter rivalry.

The facade of the Florentine church of Santa Maria Novella (completed 1470), where Alberti also intervened on behalf of the Rucellai, famously charts this transformation of ideas, with Gothic arches near the ground level of an original 13th-century elevation, and higher up, his classical

Ancient Forum, Rome, Italy.

In its suspended ruined state, the Foro Romano – with its earliest parts dating back to around the 8th century BC – still captures the need for a civilisation to visualise its mythical narratives, which are all the more seductive since they have to be rediscovered through the mists of archaeology and conjecture.

pilasters and a magnificent simplified pediment. Here the classical narrative of a harmonious rediscovered world had a new invigorating power. While it drew on past glories, it enabled a degree of order and refinement absent from most medieval buildings. More importantly it provided a readymade narrative vocabulary with which Florence could give substance to its cultural, political and ethical ideals. As though reversing the process of ruination, Alberti completed the retrospective Gothic foundation of this facade with visionary forward-looking classicism.

According to the evidence, in ancient Rome they were good at lacing buildings with narrative. As if postmodern – or should I say post-classical – in their own time, ancient Romans looked backwards and eastwards towards their cultural forebears, to Egypt and Greece. Many of their finest sculptures are based on now-lost Greek originals; in every Roman territory, buildings complied with Greek prototypes. Architects and sculptors relished enlarging and improving Greek models, and investing them with a mythological aura. On a visit to the Forum in Rome, it is not difficult to picture the intensity of this place as it was: with every conceivable deity housed in its temples, political life in its courts and palaces, fruits of the empire in the markets, and triumphant routes marked by massive arches and columns. Conversely, in every imperial outpost, an engineer's precision imposed infrastructure, militaristic control and enslavement. Architecture was understood as both organiser and communicator, and was used to the full. Even today the ruins of the Forum stack narrative high. Within this now museumised, cordoned off enclave, terraces are still laden with craggy remains and truncated columns. Outside the modern fence containing it, traffic thunders along the Viale dei Fori Imperiali, past snack vans and modern gladiators in leggings and trainers. The modern tourist city has built this heritage into its mythology.

The Roman emperor Hadrian (AD 76–138) provided perhaps the first example of a consciously narrative disposition of buildings, spaces and landscapes that freely represent faraway places. In a bid to protect himself from the tumult of Rome itself, he remodelled landscapes experienced on campaigns in the Middle East, and rebuilt them in miniature at his villa a few kilometres outside the capital at Tivoli. His objective was not only to build an isolated compound at a comfortable distance from the city, but also to reconnect it to places that otherwise would have been consigned to memory.

It was many centuries later that Tivoli proved an inspiration for a group of British designers. In the early half of the 18th century, William Kent (c 1685–1748) and his followers discovered the Arcadian narrative of evocative decline at Tivoli, and how it corresponded to the cultural and social aspirations of the owners of some of England's country houses. At

Chiswick House in West London (built and landscaped to Kent's designs in 1726–9) and Rousham in Oxfordshire (a Jacobean mansion with 1738–41 extensions and landscaping by Kent), the gardens needed to at least match the invention of the house, if not surpass it. The makers of

William Kent, Rousham House landscaping, Oxfordshire, England, 1738–41: garden and stream.

Not only do classical moments occur in strategic slopes and clearings, but the visitor is guided by a flowing stream only a few inches wide; an artery for the life force that flows through the entire garden.

William Kent, Rousham
House landscaping,
Oxfordshire, England,
1738–41: garden bower.

In a subtle half-stated
choreography, our own spirit
comes face to face with the
gods themselves. Apollo
blends perfectly with the
picturesque qualities that
Kent was after.

such environments were not so impressed by the Cartesian framework of
Versailles or Hampton Court, the perfection of which was no match for the
romantic sense of abandonment to be found in the ruins of ancient Rome
or the villas in nearby Frascati. Their decadent state heightened the sense
of rediscovery. Kent must have felt a privileged connection to a past golden
age of culture, artistry and thinking that matched his modern aspirations.
The pleasure of ruins far outshone the French taste for geometry. His
apparently found (though usually new) *objets trouvés* took the form of
tombs, temples and statuary. These could be re-discovered by the visitor or
the owner every time he took a stroll in the garden, as if stumbling across a
piece from antiquity only partly visible above the ground.

Rousham's landscape garden orchestrates a romantic literary score
with mythical fragments paced out in the woods. Here clearings and
bowers of a particularly verdant English kind collude to draw the visitor
through a variety of contrasting situations. Since they are never visible
simultaneously, and even though they are fixed in space, they succeed in
evoking a sense of the unique moment. Unlike the tightly packed buildings
of the city, Rousham's network of narrative components has a looseness

that is conducive to the work of the imagination in its quest for the sublime experience.

Stretched along a deceptively narrow strip of sloping woodland, it exploits its location to dramatic yet intimate effect. Essentially it is organised around an upper and lower path that interconnect in several clearings with pools, channels and statuary portraying mythological incidents. The visitor's first Roman encounter is with statues representing the Imperial games. Returning to the woods, a path leads to the so-called Venus Vale, with statues of Pan, a faun, and Venus. In another glade, a terrace overlooking the river is named the Praeneste after the ancient temple complex in the modern town of Palestrina outside Rome.

Although subtle in its use and occupation of the landscape, this garden fuses its storytelling with its abundant English flora. For the conceptual art commentator Simon Pugh, Rousham reinforces the role of the visitor in its system of eye catchers, paths and manipulations of nature.[5] It is a highly tuned spatial instrument for bodily and perceptual awareness that would be hard to match in the confusing and overloaded context of a city.

Narrative and the city consciousness

If in Britain we saw the use of narrative begin as a countryside sensibility in the 18th century, by the 20th century it was more strongly embedded as an urban experience. This desire to imitate literary landscapes suited the English, whose approach to power had by the mid-18th century evolved into a gentlemanly language that listened as well as commanded. Their picturesque and random nature enabled British cities to retain some sense of naturalistic mystery. Despite the shock caused by infrastructures imposed to accommodate the needs of the new industrial age, these cities had enshrined the randomness of nature in their matrices of parks, squares and gardens. London, particularly in the well-to-do west, was a loose fusion of development and parkland that had once been hunting grounds well before the invention of the Garden City at the end of the 19th century.

Although many ideals were sought in an idealised version of nature, by the late 19th century capital cities like London or Paris were acquiring a temperament of their own. The search for the sublime could be fulfilled amongst the grime, confusion and big crowds of the burgeoning city. There was a prevailing notion, expounded by the French poet Charles Baudelaire (1821–67), that the congested urban environment could trigger a bewildering and poetic state of mind which could be accessed through the technique of soaking up impressions of the city while wandering.[6] The *flâneur* – a 'paradigmatically male stroller who, equipped with his encyclopaedic knowledge of the city and its denizens, travels incognito through the most varied milieus' – could be both voyeur and participant.[7]

In the early years of the 20th century the Italian Futurists were able to blend this bewildering impression of crowds with the galvanising effect of the machine. These seething masses might have been shoppers on Christmas Eve, an audience leaving the theatre and mingling with people on the already teeming streets, or indeed troops caught in the smoke and confusion of battle. Later, the Situationist International, a predominantly French art and political movement based on Marxist principles that was formed in 1957 and dissolved in 1972, would advocate the undertaking of the *dérive* – a technique of urban wandering which, as cultural commentator Tom McDonough has observed, has its roots in the poetic *flânerie* practised by Baudelaire and other 19th-century inhabitants of the metropolis.[8]

The intensity of urban growth during the 19th century also accentuated the development of the urban park, a place designed for strolling, albeit as respite from (rather than joining up with) the urban throng.

Antoni Gaudí, Parc Güell, Barcelona, Spain, 1900–14.

A master of illusion, Gaudí brought all his skills to bear on his landscape masterpiece. To stimulate the imagination, he exaggerated an already dramatic topography with artificial terraces, decaying structures and fabulous creatures.

A Garden in the Sky . . .

One of the world's wonders—the unique Derry Roof Gardens—
some 1½ acres, 100 ft. above ground level, with green lawns,
shady trees; a flowing stream and waterfall; and several distinct
types of garden (such as the Tudor and Spanish Gardens) which
are perfect examples of their kind. Open during the fine weather
months in aid of charity. Lunches, teas and refreshments in the
Sun Restaurant.

Visitors to London
Welcome to Kensington

LONDON'S FINEST SHOPPING CENTRE

BARKERS, DERRYS and PONTINGS welcome you to the historic and
beautiful district of Kensington. These three great stores, whose gracious
buildings dominate the main thoroughfare, offer a shopping service which, in
the opinion of many, is unequalled in the Kingdom.

─TAX-FREE SHOPPING─
for OVERSEAS VISITORS
who may buy free of purchase
tax under the Personal Export
Scheme (and the Coupon Scheme
for U.S.A. & Canada) including
specially reserved goods.
Enquire for the Export Bureau.

*Six Restaurants. Buses from all districts. Underground to Kensington High Street Stn. (Inner Circle).
B.E.A. Air Station almost opposite. (A few minutes from Earl's Court and Olympia Exhibitions)*

Derrys | BARKERS | Pontings
OF KENSINGTON

KENSINGTON HIGH STREET. LONDON. W.8

xxix

Ralph Hancock, Derry
& Toms roof garden,
Kensington, London,
England, 1936–8.

Cosmopolitan cities like
London wanted to connect
with exotic experiences
available abroad, an
ambition that went well with
the efforts of department
stores to bring the Empire
to every shopper. Six storeys
above the ground, this
Alhambra in miniature would
provide a break from the
bustle below.

Many of these, like the Royal Parks in London and Central Park in New York, went to elaborate efforts to imitate nature, if in an innocuous form. But when Antoni Gaudí (1852–1926) was commissioned by the Güell family to design a public park on a steeply sloping site in the north-eastern Gràcia district of Barcelona, he wanted to inject fantasy into people's idea of nature. Like Italian hilltop towns and Rousham before it, Parc Güell (1900–14), Gaudí's landscape masterpiece, made clever use of the dramatic topography.

The slopes provided the opportunities for a variety of interlacing terraces, with meandering paths, projecting roofs and incongruous plazas that offset nature with a vibrant fantasticality. Gaudí used tried-and-tested landscape techniques in which a network of paths activates a variety of experiences, but he also incorporated so many artificial natures that real nature paled into a supporting role. The manmade was to collude with the visitors to outdo nature with the bizarre – including stairs with giant reptiles, roofs with shell-like stalagmites, and colonnades that had apparently been eroded over millennia. And everywhere there are suggestions of social gathering that could never correspond to reality: a plaza defined by large stone spheres, an undulating bench covered in his hallmark broken tiles, and beneath it, a cavernous space where giants would feel more at home than mortals. In Parc Güell mythical time and real time coincide on a daily basis. In these ultra-imaginative surroundings, relationships are free to coalesce.

A later public garden in London further detaches reality by imaginatively sampling various iconic garden types from around the world. In the inter-war period, a narrative of health-obsessed existentialism was a back note to Modernism, while a new determination to consume went hand in hand with Hollywood escapism and Art Deco extravagance. In the spirit of Britain's vast empire, Derry & Toms department store would bring the exotic Spanish garden to Kensington in West London. The roof was exploited not as a piece of antiquity, but much more exotically, as a Mediterranean garden based on the Alhambra, although it also included Tudor and British woodland gardens. Created in 1936–8 by landscape architect Ralph Hancock (1893–1950) on the instructions of store owner Trevor Bowen, this extravaganza of geometric pools, ogee arcades and leafy walks unfolded a trans-story as light relief from the intense activity of shopping. Once you'd made your purchases, you could pretend to leave the country in a loose cinematic experience of places few people could ever hope to see. And what did it matter? No one quite believed that it was any more real than the interior of an Alhambra-styled cinema. At Derry's Roof Gardens you could have tea and cakes in exotic surroundings, and then wander freely in a living movie set. Like the picture palaces, it stimulated the imagination by immersing the visitor in an otherwise inaccessible world. Being aware of the illusion was part of the experience.

Narrative as an architectural pursuit

The narrative of flight translates well into pure structure. Though an engineer, Pier Luigi Nervi (1891–1979) inspired many with his soaring naturalistic structures, including his exact contemporary Giò Ponti (1891–1979) with whom he collaborated on the Pirelli Tower (1960) in Milan. But it took an émigré American to fully engage the flight narrative in an airport building,

Eero Saarinen, Trans World Flight Center, John F Kennedy International Airport, New York, USA, 1962.

Post-war advances in engineering triggered much more invention when it came to the architectural envelope. Long before brands had any direct effect on buildings, the sweeping structure of TWA's terminal suggested that the glamour and excitement of flying began on the ground.

and make full use of the 1950s' glamour that went with it. In the Trans World Flight Center at New York's John F Kennedy International Airport (1962), the Finnish-born architect Eero Saarinen (1910–61) applied concrete shell construction to expressing the aeronautical experience. Every TWA passenger would begin or end their journey in this building. These previously unachievable soaring curves are not only eagle-like; they suggest flight itself in their trajectories. Flying while still earthbound, the structure keys the experience of the city into the system of airports and aircraft that completes an international and inter-urban reach which, by the 1960s, was becoming a reality. Here engineering and artful aspiration combine with elegance and an unrestrained libido for modernity.

On the smaller domestic scale, landscape assumes a different meaning in which narrative can be used just as effectively. As in Gaston Bachelard's seminal work on the psychological effects of the house, *The Poetics of Space* (1958), Frederick Kiesler (1890–1965) was interested in giving form to the liberated state of mind that had been unlocked by Sigmund Freud (1856–1939). To both, the house was a complex three-dimensional container of all our dreams and fears. Kiesler, a multi-talented Austrian-American iconclast, theoretician, architect and theatre designer, spent much of his career designing spaces that had a sense of time as well as place. In his Endless House – never built, but influential nevertheless after being exhibited in maquette form at the Museum of Modern Art, New York

Frederick Kiesler, Endless House, large model, 1959.

Though never realised, this exercise in psychological formation challenged the tenets of Modernism, applying Freudian thinking free from the conventions of walls, roofs and floors. The inhabitant would be able to wander from room to room as the mind shifts from thought to thought.

in 1959 – he wanted to realise a building that you could inhabit as if it were your own body: 'man and his environment are caught up in a total system of reciprocal relationships'.[9] Elevated on stilts, its loops and interstices are uncompromisingly curvaceous and body-like. Moving from 'room to room', you would leave one psychological space and, although physically entering another, there would be a lingering trace of the one you had occupied only moments earlier.

Right-leaning Italian writer Curzio Malaparte (1898–1957) wanted his home to express his own supremacy. Hardly flowing in its elongated pier-like formation, the Casa Malaparte (1938–42) sits on a rocky outcrop on the eastern side of Capri looking out to sea. The original designs for the house were provided by architect Adalberto Libera (1903–63), but Malaparte reputedly rejected them and built it himself with the help of local stonemasons. If Kiesler's house is all about flow, Malaparte's Rationalist villa is all about the eye of its owner. Even today its stacked spaces have a pervasive air of control; guests stay in cells below stairs rather than bedrooms. His lovers would stay in the room next to his, but his room alone had access to his study which is in a commanding position on the 'prow' of the building with the best view out to sea. Neither Kiesler nor any of his contemporaries were searching for this degree of compartmentalisation; indeed, the opposite.

An architect who had a more liberated – and even libertine – agenda is the Torinese polymath and late Surrealist, Carlo Mollino (1905–73). As

Curzio Malaparte and Adalberto Libera, Casa Malaparte, Capri, Italy, 1938–42.

At first this remarkable house appears to comply with Rationalist principles, but everything about it is perverse or inverted: while the entrance stair leads to an expansive sundeck, the house, complete with cell-like guest rooms, is buried beneath it.

an architect and furniture designer he put his skills to good use in his tiny *garçonnières*. They were louche spaces to be shared with no one but his partner for the night. The Casa Devalle (1939) in Turin is an essay in erotic staging on a domestic scale. In the spirit of sensual performance, this complex of intricate spaces constructs a playground of shapes, textures and functions. Every piece has stereoscopic consequences, with mirrors at angles, deep shadows and clever combinations of objects that encourage role-reversal. Mollino was a master at the body-narrative replete with erogenous zones.

Also a great racing driver and pilot, Mollino managed to load his work with every one of his interests. He was unusually skilled at expressing anthropomorphic movement, in his buildings of course, but perhaps more eloquently through his furniture. His architecture shows a Modernist vocabulary in a state of transformation towards dynamic abstraction with an extraordinary level of taste and harmony. The dynamic models evident in his furniture had the potential to be applied to much larger structures; even

Carlo Mollino, Casa Devalle, Turin, Italy, 1939.

Mollino's furniture is well known for its body-like tension, but his small apartments were equally inventive. Multi-layered, multi-textured and conceived as chambers of seduction, this *garçonnière* fuses Surrealism with clean modern economy.

though he was a pilot, he was more interested in the hedonism of flying than in looking at the city as though it were itself an object.

My last example takes us momentarily into travels of the mind. Not long after the optimistic Americanisation of Europe in the 1950s, some like Kiesler were more interested in how architecture could be a vehicle for a more personal journey. There had been numerous calls to arms in a string of passionate manifestoes occurring throughout the 20th century, but architect Ettore Sottsass (1917–2007) frequently held architecture at arm's length. Yet he constantly adhered to the discipline by testing it against every other conceivable medium – photography, ceramics, furniture and of course his famous red Valentine typewriter (designed for Olivetti in 1969).

Ettore Sottsass, 'The Planet as Festival', *Study for a Temple for Erotic Dances*, 1972–3.

In the wake of the counter-culture revelations of the 1960s, architects everywhere considered dropping out as a serious option. Sottsass spent long periods in India, and translated his experiences into totemic architecture that described a state of mind.

Far from the cosmopolitan conditions that had inspired much of the architecture of the 20th century, by the early 1970s Sottsass had turned towards ideal imaginary forms with a self-sustained temple-like singularity. Influenced by the counter-culture thinking of the 1960s, Sottsass 'tripped out' on an introspective hippie otherworldly vision. The series of drawings known as 'The Planet as Festival' (1972–3) depicts architecture as totems and evokes a utopian land in which human consciousness is awakened through freedom from work and chores and the use of technology to heighten self-awareness. Firmly rooted in the imagination, and deliberately detached from any idea of context, these are experiments in a spiritual form of travel that, despite the freedom, retain complete control. His architect's sense of social responsibility had moved on to a higher artistic plane.

To move the concept of the city forward, some architects began to stand back from it. Only then could they translate the complex post-industrial decay that by the late 1970s had enveloped the Western metropolis. The demise of traditional industries, coupled with new ways of distributing goods that took warehousing out of urban centres, had resulted in a Postmodern form of urban decline that left many buildings devoid of purpose and vast areas eerily abandoned. There was room for an approach to architecture that would ultimately eclipse functionalist ideology.

Narrative as an architectural methodology

Though always designed according to economic or functional criteria – even when they overshoot or fall short of them – clearly not all buildings are designed with the intention of narrating. Social relationships rarely outshine commercial interests. Every client has a set of expectations, including what they want their building to convey to the broader public; but the architect–client relationship depends hugely on a closed system of engagement, often leaving the effect on the public to planning and consultation. Sadly the interests of the public are relatively marginal compared with the needs of the employees or the image of the business to be housed.

But the work of architecture can be a vehicle for this narrative layer and has the potential to engage human experience in ways that mere style does not; architects who work with narrative will be aware of all these possibilities, and the need to project ideas towards the viewer through the 'medium' of architecture. On the one hand the physical nature of architecture makes it comparable to the physical object of a book, which sits between the author and the reader. On the other hand, buildings can be invested with narrative content by the architect in ways that are only possible through the medium of space. Having both substance and void, content and relations, space is a medium ready to soak up associative meaning.

Whether the end result is to be an entire neighbourhood or the reconfiguration of a room, narrative can indeed set the design process in motion. Narrative is not an option selected from a pattern book or looked up on the Internet. It relies on your ability to draw on the world around you, and render it light enough to move into the territory of the imagination – and what English writer and critic John Ruskin (1819–1900) termed an 'associative imagination' at that.[10] In the next chapter, I will investigate the seeds of narrative in the semiotic sense, and how over the 20th century experiments by some artist-architects into the language of cities laid out the territory for narrative to become a modus operandi in its own right.

References

1 Umberto Eco, 'Function and Sign: the Semiotics of Architecture', in Neil Leach (ed), *Rethinking Architecture*, Routledge (London), 1997, p 184.
2 Joseph Rykwert, *On Adam's House in Paradise, the Idea of the Primitive Hut in Architectural History*, MIT Press (Cambridge, MA), second edition, 1981.
3 Eco, op cit, p 183.
4 Official website of Palazzo Rucellai, http://www.palazzorucellai.eu/rucellai/eng/palace.html (accessed 28 June 2011).
5 Simon Pugh, 'Nature as a Garden: A Conceptual Tour of Rousham', *Studio International*, Volume CLXXXVI (1973), p 121.
6 See: Walter Benjamin, 'On some motifs in Baudelaire', in *Illuminations*, Schocken Books (New York), 1969, p 168.
7 Tom McDonough, 'Introduction', in *The Situationists and the City*, Verso (London), 2009, p 11.
8 Ibid.
9 *Frederick Kiesler: Artiste-architecte*, exhibition catalogue, Editions du Centre Pompidou (Paris), 1996, p 167.
10 John Ruskin, *Modern Painters*, Volume II, Smith, Elder & Co (London), 1846, passim.

2

Radical Terrain

The overwhelming evidence is that more people want to live in cities than ever before. By 2006 for the first time more people lived in megacities than not.[1] There are practical and survivalist reasons for this. As well as being places of production and commerce, they are eternally fascinating for being larger than ourselves, and beyond individual command. Their risk of uncertainty and danger is easily outweighed by the promise of opportunity. If the ideal of the home revolves around comfort and family cohesion, the open-ended world of the city is, relatively speaking, without limits. It satisfies the need for repetition, but also the urge to encounter the unknown, to combine the well rehearsed with the unpredictable.

As Baudelaire had discovered, cities are both spatial and atmospheric, and give structure and shape to experience. The process of familiarisation with any one urban environment requires endlessly complex and risky experiment, with every main route encountered deepened by experiments in wandering, or what the Situationists called *dérive*. These are the experiences that compose narrative patterns, and help make up the mental maps which, like a taxi driver, chart sequences in space that correspond to certain periods, days or time spent with particular people. With every journey you are inclined to construct a story in which you are both protagonist and audience.

Architects and urban strategists need to be acutely aware of how people interact with their output. Without being psychologists or cognitive theorists themselves, inevitably architects are limited to propagating their ideas through the physical environment. However, a narrative approach to architecture suggests a familiar dialogue between the physical and the phenomenal, and discovering how each can be found in the other. For example, when the architect refers to the programme, he or she is not merely referring to a set of static attributes conceived around the use to which a building will be put, but to a dynamic set of uses that constitutes a loosely configured map.

Traditionally the building gives shape to the programme, and the skill of the architect lies in the translation of this hypothetical configuration of human activity into an actual construction. But that is the dumb way of designing, and one that eschews cultural and behavioural complexities. Whether in art, movies or even the sciences, forward thinkers look to what already exists to understand how to project towards the future.

Phenomenological interpretations of the city

The same is true for architects and architectural theorists like Jane Jacobs (1916–2006) and Kevin Lynch (1918–84), whose phenomenological interpretation of cities enabled a more dynamic experience – based on understanding – than the Modernist zoning-style of planning that preceded it. While the Futurists were themselves energised by the dynamic qualities of crowds, in his influential book, *The Image of the City*, Lynch explicitly evokes the experience of moving along an urban route: 'Observers are impressed, even in memory, by the apparent "kinaesthetic" quality of a path, the sense of motion along it: turning, rising, falling. Particularly this is true where the path is traversed at high speed. A great descending curve which approaches a city center can produce an unforgettable image.'[2] From here it is only a short step to Robert Venturi's (b 1925) observation that on the highway, often the sign dwarfs the architecture, and in terms of signification, replaces it. Although driven by the dynamic effects of the metropolis, Lynch still stresses the visual, with the city complying with a combination of elemental archetypes – path, edge, district, node and landmark – that are arranged in 'a multi-purpose, shifting organization, a tent for many functions'.[3]

Although conceived as an efficient rationally functioning organism, the city combines a myriad of experiences that were never intended by any of its makers; it constitutes a complex interlaced compost of casually arranged organic rejects – or, as British-American architectural theorist Colin Rowe (1920–99) would have said, a rich combination of *objets trouvés* that jostle for position as a result of politics and history.[4] It is the very impenetrability of this agglomeration that makes it available to multiple interpretation and the formation of memories. Most people agree that their earliest memories stem from around the age of four, and might recall a context, a situation. In growing up you learn to measure your own body against the world, and to learn by constantly testing and reassuring. In turn, as Freud observed, 'consciousness comes into being in the site of a memory trace'.[5] Memories accumulate in language and experience, and both are constantly challenged by the desire to transgress, and penetrate the unknown.

According to French philosopher Maurice Merleau-Ponty (1908–61), 'Our own body is in the world as the heart is in the organism: it keeps the visible spectacle constantly alive, it breathes life into it and sustains it inwardly, and with it forms a system.'[6] This suggests a gradually deepening awareness of individual presence in the world, which is further contextualised by attractive and repulsive experiences. Despite an inbuilt resistance to traumatic memories, Freud's *mémoire involontaire* contrasts with the positive framework expressed in the work of highly influential French writer Marcel Proust (1871–1922) that sees the environment as an elaborate backdrop to events. Much of the work of the avant-garde consists of manipulating these phenomena, and finding ways to interpret otherwise hidden aspects of our

Guy Debord, *The Naked City* (lithograph on paper), 1957.

Typical of Situationist technique, this iconic image was one of a series in which Debord cut the arrondissements of Paris from one another and rearranged them to suggest a much more immediate and dynamic kind of urban geography.

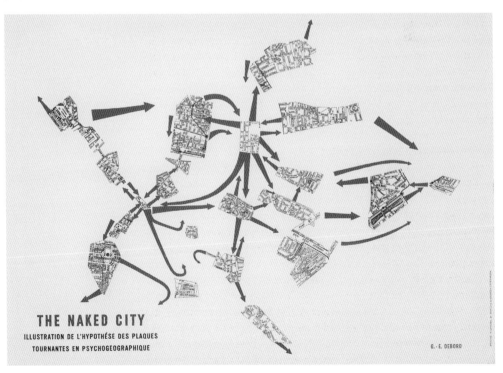

THE NAKED CITY

ILLUSTRATION DE L'HYPOTHÉSE DES PLAQUES
TOURNANTES EN PSYCHOGEOGRAPHIQUE

G.-E. DEBORD

environment, dredging up forgotten memories and re-contextualising them.

Guy Debord (1931–94), the leading light of the Situationist International, began to produce images of Paris based on cut-up maps, in which the arrondissements were rearranged to make a scrambled alternative geography. Combining fragments with an overlay of red arrows, they emphasise urban flow at the expense of the logical disposition of streets and buildings. The most iconic of these, *The Naked City* (1957), is part factual and part experiential. The message is that citizens should not take the city at face value, but deconstruct it, making space for their own existence as well as for those hostile forces within it. By casting a radial artistic eye, it expresses the city in a revolutionary pictorial form, a narrative 'poetic' form, and as such becomes an instrument of cultural transgression. As is so often the case, it takes an artist, and not an architect, to show us how to interpret our surroundings.

As Tom McDonough observes:

> *Dérive* was at some essential level, the search for an encounter with otherness, spurred on in equal parts by the exploration of pockets of class, ethnic and racial difference in the post-war city, and by frequent intoxication ... However, for the Situationists these (psychogeographic) plans cannot be reduced to a purely individual response to the urban terrain; cities were for them profoundly historical landscapes, whose current appearances were shaped – as geological strata underlay physical landscapes – by the successive events that time had buried, though never completely effaced.[7]

Members of the Situationist International, and in particular their one architect Constant Nieuwenhuys (1920–2005), had been searching for a physical environment that matched their hopes for a culturally, sexually and politically liberated society. Not unlike the experiments by Kiesler and Saarinen, in 1953 Constant embarked on his *New Babylon* projects (which would endure until 1974), to discover what he hoped would be a new form of urbanism. These exuberant models emphasised loose connections between the functional parts. Again lifted from the ground on stilts, his visions for cities are in fact paradigms of the existing city in all its haphazard connection and confluence as expressed in some of the group's psychogeographic diagrams.

The reach of the Situationists is still felt today; much avant-garde work in architecture replays the subversive procedures so consciously performed by Debord and his comrades. What has become clear is that two threads of influence evolved side by side. The first of these looked to

Constant Nieuwenhuys,
New Babylon, 1974.

In his search for a liberated
kind of urbanism, Constant
made hundreds of models
and drawings, though most
were continuous structures
that hovered above the
ground; their organic
dynamism did not so much
house events as stimulate
them.

their analysis of the city as a terrain in which a variety of forces battled for
occupancy and use. From this thread sprung in the 1960s and 1970s the
work of the Florentine groups Archizoom and, in a less classically left-wing
form, Superstudio, which at times comes close to a totalitarian parody.
Further along the same trajectory sit the early work of Dutch architect Rem
Koolhaas (b 1944) and Franco-American architect Bernard Tschumi (b 1944).
A second thread takes up the performance side captured in the *dérive*. This
is the trajectory of the anarchist architect, from Hans Hollein (b 1934) and
Gianni Pettena (b 1940) via the lateral influence of filmmaker Derek Jarman
(1942–94) and pop music impresario Malcolm McLaren (1946–2010), and
later returning to architecture with my own NATO group.

Critical reflection on the prevailing culture frame is an accepted
function of contemporary art. Architects on the other hand are constrained
by the responsibility to improve on the world as they find it. Too frequently
critical observation remains exactly that without leading to its corollary, a
blueprint for what does not yet exist.

The critical and the conceptual

In hindsight, Modernism tended to repress the allegorical aspect of
architecture, preferring instead to apply the tired maxim of 'form follows
function'. It might also have added 'efficiency equals boredom', whereas
from its outset in the early 1900s, cinema built on the dynamic relationship

between fragmentary and continuous experience. It learnt to construct emotional experience through montage and assembly.

In his *Aircraft Carrier City in Landscape* project (1964), Hans Hollein, the Austrian maverick and in the early 1970s one of the biggest influences on the architectural avant-garde across the world, simultaneously evoked and undermined Utopia in one visually arresting stroke. The image of the aircraft carrier atop a gently rolling landscape carries all of its original power today. Hollein made no attempt to disguise the identity of the vessel, but by recontextualising it on land, he instantly converted it into architecture. The mathematical balance between this absurd idea and the frankness of the image render it iconic.

Gianni Pettena, one of the so-called Radical Architects, emerged from the atrophied architectural education system offered by Florence University in the late 1960s. His 'Anarchitecture' took its cues from performance art, Gordon Matta-Clark's urban actionism and the new currency of Arte Povera. He implemented many of his early works in America: 'In my visits to the USA I was a voyeur I suppose. I was in love with funk architecture, and the work of the hippies in the shape of the handmade house. I was not particularly attracted to the US but to the culture of my generation.'[8] His Ice

Gianni Pettena,
Unconscious Architecture,
1972–3.

Many of the Italian radicals were drawn to the USA by the music, the lifestyle and the image of freedom. Pettena found a pre-existing architecture in the great outcrops of Colorado's Monument Valley, photographed them and organised them with an architect's eye for type.

Hans Hollein, *Aircraft Carrier City in Landscape*, perspective, 1964 (unbuilt).

A tantalising yet inscrutable object as work of architecture. The iconic status of the aircraft carrier made it all the more mysterious and iconoclastic in this unlikely landscape setting.

Houses in Minneapolis (1971–2), for which water was poured over buildings overnight and allowed to freeze into a solid block; his Clay House in Salt Lake City (1972), comprising a small house covered in hand-spread clay; and his documenting of Colorado's Monument Valley in *Unconscious Architecture* (1972–3), which sought to provide a bona fide interpretation of rocky outcrops as the temples of the Navaho people – all of these equally meet, and negate, the architectural object. Like projection onto buildings, Pettena's works take existing objects in the world, and convert them. Unlike iconic architecture, they take what might otherwise be overlooked and enable it to be seen architecturally.

Indeed, many architects valued their conceptual work more highly than the chance to build. The London-based avant-garde group Archigram, founded in the 1960s, avoided building anything, some say successfully, with the implication that to build would rob their work of its visionary power. On the other hand Superstudio seemed to envisage the future 'city' as a continuous Woodstock-style festival for the benefit of 'all' (meaning a highly restricted elite).[9] In contrast to Venturi's suggestion that Disney World is the world people really want, and not the world of architects, Superstudio saw beyond the need for any specific sense of place or circumstance. In their idealised yet ultimately dystopian society housed in a *Continuous Monument* project of 1969, there would be 'no further need for cities or castles. No further need for roads or squares. Every point will be the same as any other (excluding a few deserts or mountains which are in no way inhabitable)'.[10]

At a time of the pervasive influence of Archigram and the vibrant posse of conceptual architects that, by the late 1960s, surrounded them, Rem Koolhaas developed his Architectural Association graduation project, *Exodus* (1972). Koolhaas was fascinated by the effects of the Cold War on cities like New York, London and Moscow.[11] The radical background laid by the Russian Suprematists in the early part of the century, with their fundamentally geometric focus, had been 'interrupted'. Taking up the story where they had left off, he proposed a vast enclosure across central London into which much of the population would voluntarily migrate to be part of a freer and more ideal world within its walls. The architecture was highly compartmentalised, applying the grid that was fashionable at the time. (Hollein and Superstudio had already used it to great effect.) With further resonances of the Berlin Wall, Koolhaas's project parodied consumer society in an elaborate and ironic

Rem Koolhaas, *Exodus, or the Voluntary Prisoners of Architecture*, aerial view, 1972.

In the early 1970s vast structures on a totalitarian scale proliferated. Koolhaas's version made an east–west strip across central London; according to the elaborate narrative, citizens would be drawn to the perfect world inside its high walls.

narrative of belief in the liberties promised by youth culture. It is a total vision closer to the ambitions of a novel or a movie spanning all scales, from the broad sweep of London to the intensity of rock concerts and observation towers. With it Utopia acquired a conceptual sting in the tail that, from that moment on, prevented it from regaining the attraction it had had in the previous decade, and Communism had been reduced to a caricature long before the collapse of the Soviet Union.

Architects on the other hand have a long tradition of substantially outstretching the scale of buildings towards the city. Many have produced theoretical versions of the metropolitan condition in generic form, often a form that can be repeated ad infinitum, rolling out a coded surface that could replace any notion of natural landscape or existing urban sprawl. The seductive nature of this vision of power points towards an equivalence of social code and physical framework that might support it, and a self-satirising of Utopia that suggests an absence of narrative. While violent computer games are loaded with narrative, the *No-Stop City* project (1969)

Rem Koolhaas, *Exodus, or the Voluntary Prisoners of Architecture*, barrier rights, 1972.

Propelled by the monotony of their normal lives, citizens would queue at the gates of this dubious paradise. Having passed scrupulous inspection, they would be admitted as permanent residents in a series of compounds where perfection would be assured.

by Archizoom and Andrea Branzi (b 1938) combines a serviced landscape providing continuous protection (context) with a system of intelligent artefacts (use) and finally an egalitarian ethos (narrative).

Communism had never really provided a dense or human enough language to constitute a narrative with any colour, contrast or surprise. In this sense it was simply a counterfeit version of Modernism, in which society aped the machine. But this is exactly the attraction of *No-Stop City*. It is a parody of our hopes for a universal solution that solves societal problems once and for all. In all its care to avoid direct notions of inhabitation, it triggers a critique of the dispassion of most architectural strategies. With models repeatedly making use of infinity mirrors, there is no room for combining this thinking with the city as we know it.

This was a static 'potentialised' version of the message of the 'event' being mapped in space that Bernard Tschumi discussed in his *Manhattan Transcripts* (1981).[12] Others took a more populist drive to the architecture of their time. For Rem Koolhaas in his first major tome *Delirious New York* (1978), the builders of Manhattan capitalised on the entertainment

Archizoom, *No-Stop City*, 1969.

In an apparition of the Truman Show, Archizoom could see that an industrialised form of architecture could enable free movement, and that repetition could facilitate new kinds of social ecology.

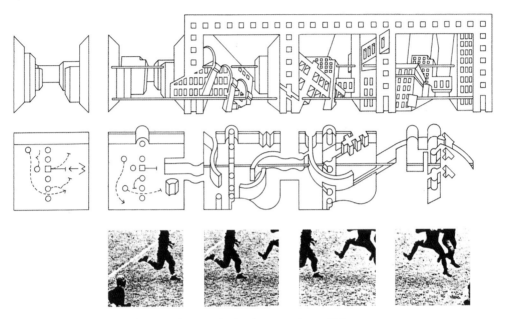

architecture of Coney Island.[13] A modern city had to be more than efficient – it had to inspire the population and the investor alike, and would take up the easiest means to enlist the popular imagination.

Bernard Tschumi, *Manhattan Transcripts*, 1976–81.

Captivated by new forms of movement notation and the documenting of performance, Tschumi mixed such diagrams with the architectural plan. The exercise resulted in a reworking of the typological diagram favoured by Rationalists like the Krier brothers.

Architecture of the event

Nowadays it is common enough to speak of the 'narrative' of a building, but how often does the term suggest any more than the idea behind the project? Could it indicate a poetic message bound up in architecture's material manifestation? Or is it a device that could hike up the degree of existential turbulence? When the term first emerged in the early 1980s it was chosen to describe a set of values. It placed the circumstances surrounding a building in a higher position than the building itself, circumscribing the 'event', as Bernard Tschumi called it, in relation to the architectural object. Tschumi drew parallels between a sequence of events in space and the physical conditions of the city. There was a need to understand the dynamics between the physical form of architecture and what happens in it, and these relations were subject to degrees of manipulation introduced by the architect.

As if to emphasise the tenuous link between them, Tschumi likened known stories, many of them archetypal like the 'story' of a football game or classic murder mystery, to the urban terrain. The narrative would engender a first-hand set of experiences rather than the emblematic shared experience normally associated with architecture. In his rhetorically driven 'Advertisements for Architecture' series of juxtaposed words and images, done while he was a tutor at the Architectural Association in 1976–7, he associated murder with architecture, and used this perceived violence to emphasise the gulf between a building's neutrality and an individual's perception of events.

Tschumi elaborated this raw confrontation with his first realised project at Parc de la Villette (1982–98), his *grand projet* park close to the northern band of the Périphérique around Paris. He wanted to find out what happened when you applied the grid to a large open surface with only a few relatively large features left over from its previous incarnation as a meat market. His competition entry cleverly combined a grid of red 'cubes' with existing features such as the canal and an enormous slaughterhouse, with a number of irregular interventions such as a covered promenade and a meandering path based on the language of film.

La Villette enabled Tschumi to explore the detachment of architecture from its function, while introducing the notion that meaning comes from

Bernard Tschumi, Parc de La Villette, Paris, France, overhead perspective with red follies, 1982.

Repetition and deviating from it begot this winning competition entry. A grid of red follies suggests the fragile order in society, while arabesque marks and meandering paths hint at the need for eccentricity.

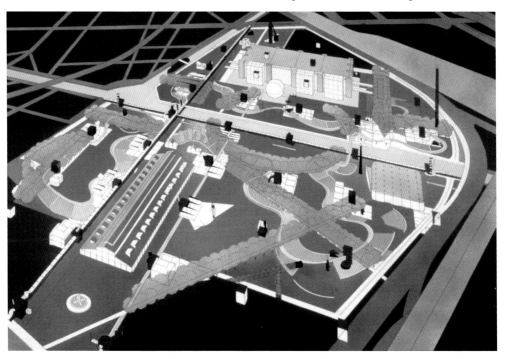

other more associative possibilities arising from the gap between the actual use of the park (strolling, football) and its symbolic use (film, architectural heritage, society). Although he resists the suggestion that the park has any direct relation to nature, preferring to see it as an abstract landscape onto which human activity can perform and interact, it is in fact a straightforward paradigm for nature as a complex layering of interdependent eco-systems, each of which possesses their own dynamics, their own drawn red arrows.

The urban and street style

Cross-platforming has become part of the language of the post-millennial generation of architects. These kinds of intervention seem to drive advertising and the media generally. Society occupies environments that have adopted rhetoric in all its forms; displacement and replacement switch their roles in every field. As cities have become increasingly multi-cultural and kaleidoscopic, it follows that art and architecture have experimented with fragmentation, taking Debord's *Naked City* to just about every commercial realm. It was on this ticket that Deconstruction emerged as a philosophy and a style in the 1990s and, along with narrative, continues to fragment programmes and typologies.

Even though sharing a common root with narrative, namely a post-Structuralist method of examining contemporary culture, Deconstruction is not the principal subject of this book; it has been extensively covered in other volumes. As Umberto Eco has said, 'What our semiotic framework would recognize in the architectural sign is the presence of a sign vehicle whose denoted meaning is the function it makes possible.'[14] But there is another dimension to meaning that is existential rather than pragmatic, and arises in getting to know the world and mapping experiences within it. At its broadest level, all spatial experience is a form of storytelling; experience and the physical environment are narrative paradigms for one another. According to American theorist Walter Fisher in his elaboration of the 'narrative paradigm', rather than organising data as facts in logical relationships, most people retain their everyday information as anecdotal narratives with characters, plots, motivations and actions.[15] However convinced of a process governed by logic or consequences, in the course of designing, designers tell stories too. We need to find out how these two spheres – the experience of architecture, and the architecture of experience – can be connected.

To make this connection I have looked to the cities I know. Of the many drivers that help shape architecture, one stands out as particular to the past two decades – an awareness of lifestyle and how people can now adapt

Protesting students in street battles with police in the rue Saint-Jacques in Paris, France, 6 May 1968.

The revolutionary spirit of the early 1960s that had arisen in the UK and the USA had changed little in France. There youth turned to politics rather than pop culture, and staged a mini-revolution. Though a traumatic attack on the bourgeoisie, the protesters were well heeled.

the city and use it as a stage for their own experiments. In an essay 'Street Signs' I wrote in 1985, I explored the influence of street style on architectural thinking.[16] Certainly in terms of fashion and music, the aesthetic of the time was to celebrate the abject and to twist signs of taste away from conventions of beauty. 'The street' provided polemical opposition to so many tenets of acceptable behaviour. Clothes were ripped and deployed badly printed images. Music was self-consciously aggressive and 'badly' performed. The backdrop for all this was an urban condition of obsolescence and decay. By the late 1970s there was a palpable awareness amongst young people of a city in ruins. In turn this realisation made way for an unprecedented looseness in interpreting the urban environment, and a lack of programmatic determinism when it came to imagining how it might work in the immediate, as yet undefined future.

The Britain of the 1970s was very much a black-and-white drama of the English kitchen-sink kind. That decade was witness to a huge jolt towards anarchic expression, in fashion and in music. Artists and proto-fashionistas roamed empty streets armed with the first (barely) portable video cameras. And with a new Walkman, you could score the city with your own soundtrack, starring in a movie-of-the-mind by merely meandering around.[17] A guerrilla mood energised most contemporary frontiers, giving rise to the particular artsy scene that resulted in Derek Jarman's film *Jubilee* (1977). With it, he stepped outside the conventions of experimental cinema, making a feature that had the potential to reach large audiences.

1970s streetscape,
London, England.

In the mid-1970s Britain's
urban landscape was even
more derelict than it had
been after the war; buildings
were still black from
accumulated soot and, apart
from pubs, there was little in
the way of entertainment.

Derek Jarman, *Jubilee*,
1977.

Jarman's *Jubilee* broke
the rules even of more
experimental filmmaking.
Using an episodic form
instead of a conventional
plot, it reflected the anarchic
and eclectic nature of 1970s'
London life.

Appearing at the height of Punk, *Jubilee* did not have a conventional plot. It is episodic in nature, with the narrative built around a number of inversions such as depositing Elizabeth I into this Elizabethan age – in which the present Queen has been assassinated, and her kingdom left to marauding proto-punks. Cars burn in abandoned streets of grim bricked-up terraces. On the inside, gangs of 'artists' live in warehouse 'lofts' that, in their eclectic assembly of booty from the streets, avoid any recognisable domestic style. The sets revelled in the unlikely union of the traditional and the provisional: a mattress on the floor next to a Louis-something armchair, a motorbike, a manifesto hurriedly daubed in black paint on the wall. It needed to avoid bourgeois connotation at all costs. Jarman reflected back with added intensity the entropic rawness of 1970s' London, and found a way of attacking the status quo with newly found irony, artistry and delight.

New York at the time was also in a state of grungy transition as the Big Apple: as it began to be marketed as dangerous and healthy at the same time, Manhattan, the destination *de rigueur*, was full of social mutations. It had turned into a living hyper-narrative of creative chaos with sordid basement clubs and after-hours lounges in abandoned cinemas. Architectural culture was pretty much nowhere in this mix. With the added ingredients of the Andy Warhol cool effect, and the burgeoning art and music scene focused around SoHo, New York's influence had resounding effects in London.

Yet back in the UK there was a peculiar art-schooly Situationism that had its own unique chemistry. Seditionaries, a boutique on the then-fashionable Kings Road, was the unlikely HQ for Punk UK style. From here Malcolm McLaren famously launched bands like the Sex Pistols and Bow Wow Wow, and his partner Vivienne Westwood dressed them in bondage pants and ripped T-shirts.

The success of the first true mega club in London, The Embassy in Bond Street (1978), had added nightlife to the already dizzy fallout of Punk. The Embassy's clean-cut bar and dance floor provided the perfect backdrop for the clientele's overt dress sense. In 1982 McLaren and Westwood went up west too with their boutique Nostalgia of Mud situated just off Oxford Street, designed by Roger Burton. Its greasy tarpaulins and suspended resin map of the world perfectly captured a postmodern narrative of heroic resistance. Meanwhile in Manchester the Hacienda Club by designer Ben Kelly played on the narrative of the street in a state of repair, and fused it with the potent

Malcolm McLaren, Nostalgia of Mud, St Christopher's Place, London, England, 1982.

By the 1980s McLaren, together with Vivienne Westwood, had parented an alternative music and fashion scene with a distinctly urban edge. With the Kings Road already safely within their grasp, they ventured into the West End with a Hillbilly look of shop and clothes to match.

Ben Kelly, The Hacienda
Club, Manchester,
England, 1982.

The street had become
a metaphor for youthful
invention, so it made perfect
sense to introduce signs of
it into the club. Kelly used
the warning signs from
roadworks to accentuate
the alchemy of music
and untamed late-night
behaviour.

music sensibility then emerging from the gritty remains of industrial cities in
the North of England.

   The newly formed urban zeitgeist was coming through loud and strong
as an accentuated lifestyle, but with no immediate connection to architectural
ideas that at that time were fixed on Post-Modernism, as elucidated by
American-born architectural theorist Charles Jencks (b 1939), and European
Rationalism, led by Italian architect Aldo Rossi (1931–97) and Luxembourgian
urban designers the Krier brothers (Rob (b 1938) and Léon (b 1946)).

   Disfiguration can evidently turn into configuration, which perhaps
explains the convoluted psychology of the graffiti artist. An inverted sense of
authorship means that the tags, the signatures, are as large as the swing of
the arm with a spray can. Graffiti aesthetics depend on a baroque-ification
of script to the point that the word becomes submerged in colour and form.
For the graffiti artist the city itself is a legitimate canvas: looking, reacting
and painting the object of constraint materialises action. In the early 1980s,
the cryptic tagging of Jean-Michel Basquiat (1960–88) as SAMO ('Same Old
Shit') appeared all over New York City. More recently London's undercover
spray artist Banksy has pushed his art to the limits; buildings turn into picture
frames for his wittily crafted visualisations of discontent.

Curating at the cutting edge

Over in the official art world, the sense of order a curator attempts to create mirrors that of the architect in the city. Collections tend to be organised according to -isms, techniques, origin or era. Grouped and re-categorised, museum objects can be compared according to all kinds of other criteria, including size, colour, artistry and style. Only rarely do museums curate according to story. Shows like 'Pier and Ocean' (1980) or 'Psycho Buildings' (2008), both at London's Hayward Gallery, have attempted an extra narrative twist that captures some of the concern for storytelling that is prevalent in BritArt. This technique has been used to organise the permanent collections at Tate Modern, which bring together art works of diverse dates, styles and origin under overarching 'narrative themes' – such as 'material gestures' or 'poetry and dream' – that help make sense of the many strands of 20th-century contemporary art.

Attributed to Banksy, spray and stencil artwork based on the 'London Calling' album cover by The Clash, opposite News International in London, 25 October 2010.

Outside the normal illegibility of graffiti, Banksy's images combine a cartoon-like clarity with a witty exploitation of context that helps recount the visceral story of the city and the opposing forces that inhabit it.

Pavement with furniture, 2006.

Eventually every dream interior has its day, and finishes up in the seething marketplace that is London. Antique arcades and bric-a-brac shops offer a mixed-up portraiture of a city in a constant state of renewal.

Though objects in museums are often placed with great deliberation, sometimes adjacencies accentuate meanings accidentally. To a certain extent cities are the same. One expects the effect of one building on another to be considered by the architect. But much of the meaning that arises in the urban environment occurs by chance. These 'accidents' sustain the roving photographer's attentive eye, and are proof that the city is always changing, and always has something unexpected to reveal. You may notice a chance encounter between second-hand items casually placed for sale on the pavement outside a shop, or a heap of rubble left behind by a demolished building. These accidental 'installations' speak volumes and are not far from works created by artists like American Minimalist Carl André (b 1935), or 'Young British Artist' Sarah Lucas (b 1962) – including the latter's *Fuck Destiny* (2000), composed of a sofa bed, fluorescent tubes, light bulbs and a wooden box. Merely in the act of noticing them, the viewer interprets the city in a narrative way.

Narrative potential

For an architect, an examination of such juxtapositions – planned and accidental – can help shape a narrative lexicon that might counteract the alienating side of cities. As we have seen, radical movements have consistently foregrounded narrative as an area ripe for investigation, highlighting the fact that design must go beyond the visual to take account of deeper issues of experience, association and belonging. A more holistic approach to these considerations offers rich potential for the discipline of architecture. In the following chapters, I explore the impact they can have on its practice, beginning with an account of how narrative came to infuse and dominate my own work and teaching from the 1980s onwards.

References

1 *World Urbanization Prospects: The 2007 Revision – Highlights*, United Nations (New York), 2007, p.2.
2 Kevin Lynch, *The Image of the City*, MIT Press (Cambridge, MA), 1960, p 97.
3 Ibid. p 109.
4 See: Colin Rowe and Fred Koetter, *Collage City*, MIT Press (Cambridge, MA; London), 1978, pp 151–81.
5 Sigmund Freud, *Beyond the Pleasure Principle*, first published in German in 1920, first English edition published in London, 1921.
6 Maurice Merleau-Ponty, *Phenomenology of Perception*, first published in French in 1945, first English edition published by Routledge & Kegan Paul (London), 1962.
7 Tom McDonough, 'Introduction', in *The Situationists and the City*, Verso (London), 2009, p 10.
8 Author's interview with Gianni Pettena on the Frecciargento train from Florence to Venice, 26 August 2010.
9 Emilio Ambasz (ed), *Italy: The New Domestic Landscape*, exhibition catalogue, Museum of Modern Art (New York), 1972.
10 Adolfo Natalini (ed), *Superstudio: Life, Education, Ceremony, Love, Death*, Neue Galerie am Landesmuseum, Joanneum (Graz, Austria), 1973.
11 See: *Cold War Modern: Design 1945–1970*, exhibition catalogue, Victoria & Albert Museum (London), 2008.
12 Bernard Tschumi, *The Manhattan Transcripts*, Academy Editions (London), 1981.
13 Rem Koolhaas, *Delirious New York: A Retroactive Manifesto for Manhattan*, Thames & Hudson (London), 1978.
14 Umberto Eco, 'Function and Sign: the Semiotics of Architecture', in Neil Leach (ed), *Rethinking Architecture*, Routledge (London), 1997, p 184.
15 Walter Fisher, 'The Narrative Paradigm: an Elaboration', *Communication Monographs*, Volume 52, Issue 4 (December 1985), pp 347–67.
16 Nigel Coates, 'Street Signs', in John Thackara (ed), *Design after Modernism: Beyond the Object*, Thames & Hudson (London), 1988, pp 95–114.
17 The Sony Walkman was introduced with a cassette tape in 1979, and with a CD in 1984.

3

NATO

Returning to London in 1981 from a year in New York, I became obsessed by a newly expressionistic art that was being shown in prominent SoHo galleries. Artists like Julian Schnabel (b 1951), Francesco Clemente (b 1952) and Sandro Chia (b 1946) had finally pushed aside Arte Povera in favour of what came to be known as the Transavantgarde. The term 'narrative painting' had also surfaced in relation to various artists who were part of gallerist Holly Solomon's stable, including Judy Pfaff (b 1946) and Izhar Patkin (b 1955). Solomon wanted to distinguish her artists' work from the dry conceptualism and performance that dominated other Manhattan art venues like The Kitchen, and the latter-day formalism of the Leo Castelli Gallery on West Broadway. In London I realised that as an architect I could throw out my Rapidograph technical pen, and 'paint' architecture with a narrative derived from the life I was leading. In the 1980s it was the degree of social dysfunction and urban decay in Britain that tipped the balance.

Like all teachers feeling their way, I tentatively introduced my hunches to students at London's Architectural Association (AA) in Diploma Unit 10, which I had taken over from Bernard Tschumi in 1978 (and continued as Unit Master until 1988). I thought: why not put the French philosophy to one side, and try drawing more freely and being lavish with colour? A bible at the time was a remaindered book, *A Tonic to the Nation*, about the 1951 Festival of Britain that we all found captivating in its crassness and optimism.[1] For Britain at least, the Festival was relatively unrestrained, with the story told by every structure blistering out into sculptures and graphics that matched the scale of

Sir Basil Spence, Sea &
Ships Pavilion, Festival of
Britain, London, England,
1947–51: exterior model.

Driven by the expressionist
side-effects of war, the
Festival of Britain was
determined to be dynamic;
the most talented young
architects and designers
joined forces to come up
with a variety of functionalist
narratives that would
galvanise recovery.

the buildings. The book featured intriguing diagrams that traced a route past
the main features of the story in each pavilion.

In the academic year 1981–2, the group of students in my unit
was getting the hang of an anarchistic working method that mixed music,
performance and film culture. Short video performances were produced
with the help of Ricardo Pais (b 1945), a Portuguese theatre director. Strange
props and outfits appeared in the 'surreal' interpretations of everyday life
that began the academic year. The overall theme was to be 'Giant-Sized
Baby Town', a title appropriated from a Bow Wow Wow song produced by
McLaren. Our goal was to visualise a new independent 'state' on the Isle of
Dogs in London's Docklands, which under Prime Minister Margaret Thatcher's
new government policy was earmarked as an enterprise zone with a loose
approach to planning, though not I suspect as free as we imagined. The idea
of the island state certainly inspired the students; it was as attractive as it was
implausible. People would live and work in the same environments. It was not
only our job to design it, but to fully communicate it, and assert it as reality.

In response to the output of the project, Tschumi observed:
'Architecture ceases to be a backdrop for actions, becoming the action itself.'[2]
This ultimate live-work world meant that people would literally live – sleep,
eat and bathe – in facilities built around, above and below the production
line. New meanings were emerging anyway for British industry; factories

Simeon Halstead, Wine Dispenser, Architectural Association, London, England, 1982.

An early experiment with the students was the creation of an object that combined art and science. Everyone instinctively knew that the more obtuse the function, the greater the potential for the video that was to follow.

were becoming a thing of the past and were a legitimate condition for students to reinvent. We wanted to cross-reference storyboards, sections through large parts of the city, and the production line. Montage, as clashing situations were called in film theory, could be the result of an environmental 'assemblage' that brings several modes of thinking together into one linear (con)fusion that combines 'event, movement and space'.[3]

With Tschumi I had some experience in publishing with some small end-of-year books at the AA. The most significant among these was the catalogue accompanying an exhibition organised at the Royal College of Art in 1975 by curator RoseLee Goldberg called 'A Space: A Thousand Words'. In this, some twenty-eight artists' and architects' artworks consisted of exactly that: an image and a text presented as a single work. It was good grounding perhaps for the more Punk-oriented mood of the early 1980s. If we had published then it would have been close to some of the earlier Situationist publications from the 1960s. We were fulfilling Situationist International member Attila Kotányi's (1924–2004) call to arms: 'A little handbook of appropriated (détourné) vocabulary should be developed. I am suggesting that, sometimes, instead of reading neighbourhood we read: gangland.

Instead of social organisation: protection. Instead of society: racket. Instead of culture: conditioning. Instead of leisure: protected crime. Instead of education: premeditation.'[4]

The following year the focus shifted to another part of London's Docklands: Surrey Docks on the south side of the Thames, around Bermondsey and Rotherhithe. Thatcher's cavalier politics had encouraged me to think up ironic forms of imperial power as captured by the Falklands War. The war dominated the media from its beginning on 2 April 1982 until long after it was over by mid-June. The first project I set for the new group was a Museum of the Falklands War. I wanted to do the project at the same time as everyone else. It would encourage a paint-in and lots of work done very fast.

The site was an ancient flight of outdoor stairs down to the river's edge called Globe Stairs. Despite their modest scale in relation to the size of London, they captured the absurdity of a war over a small group of islands off the coast of Argentina. Mark Prizeman (b 1959) did some enormous drawings of converted battleships moored at an inlet in the Thames. In my version of the project, HMS *Albion*, one of Her Majesty's returning warships, would be converted to house a permanent re-enactment of the destruction of the Argentine warship the *General Belgrano*. A stair `of flames' would lead up to an exhibition capsule from which a sculpture of a sacrificed sailor would hover above the building. All technical description in the drawing had given way to an expressionistic capturing of the moment, and the effect on the viewer. To build such a thing you would need to work backwards from the drawings.

This experiment was followed by the customary mini projects of constructed object, performance and video, and eventually the group began to look at the larger area of Surrey Docks. This time I wanted them to mix up art and science, and explore the effects on these worn-out and run-down parts of London. The word 'anarchy' was rarely used, but there was an anything-goes spirit behind much of the work. We competed to see who could come up with the most bizarre scenarios, yet somehow they were all related to the city as we found it. It appeared to be an aspiration for the younger generation of society that we should live fearlessly, and that the city return to a primal state without any imperial delusions. Power should be in the hands of the people, and indeed it was if you had a video camera.

That year much of the work fizzed with the attitude of the people we imagined would inhabit our projects. It was a premonition of the cultural buzz that would begin to take shape ten years later in Hoxton, just north of central London. But to critics of the time its lifestyle scenario-building was dangerously remote from the conventions of architectural design. Plans

Nigel Coates, Falklands Museum 1 and 2, 1982 (unbuilt). (Right and overleaf)

A first project for the Architectural Association's newly recruited Unit 10 was a museum to bring events of the recent war alive for visitors. The site was Globe Stairs near the Surrey Docks. In my version of the project, HMS *Albion* was converted into the museum; an Exocet strike would be frozen into stairs leading up to a circular gallery above the Thames.

Mark Prizeman, *Albion*, 1983.

Many of the AA's Unit 10 students revelled in the possibilities of a city in a permanent state of entropy. Here a dreary council block has been adorned with some spirited additions and a mugging is taking place on an aerial walkway; discarded handbags from such events are piled into a heap to one side of a local greyhound track.

and sections had mostly disappeared in favour of a lurid form of illustration that accompanied the elaborate 'stories' which manifested the workings of each particular part of the city under scrutiny by each student. Although it wasn't formally narrative in the sense that there were plots and story lines with a beginning and an end, this work was certainly as narrative as the work of Holly Solomon's artists. It was full of imaginary content, character and portraiture of the people who would live in it. It was about burgeoning, misbehaving and occasional criminal society that in our view was closer to the reality of London than were the families with children clutching balloons that appeared in most 'artists' impressions' of the mediocre buildings that were actually being built.

Some very strong projects emerged, including Christina Norton's *Marriage Line*, Robert Mull's *Parliament*, Simeon Halstead's *Resort* and Mark Prizeman's *Wolf Housing*.[5] Each of them evolved a lifestyle premise, and applied it as literally and as assertively as possible to a sectional slice taken more or less arbitrarily through the city fabric. We were all convinced

Mark Prizeman, *Wolf Housing*, 1983.

The socially minded designs of the 1970s have been given a new twist with a housing project with a wolf run on the roof. Unlike Le Corbusier's ideal of a park on top of the building, Prizeman makes the housing and roof hostile to one another.

by the collective reality of our project and, negotiating the edges between its constituent parts done by different authors, discovered that conflicts could be turned to advantage. Similarly the decrepit shadows of the area's former glory found their way into much of the work. Existing sheds or tower blocks were readily retained, and gave a punky layering to the outcome. For instance, Mark Prizeman 'converted' a tower block of police flats into a new housing project that included some of the East End's more borderline entertainments, like dog racing and handbag snatching.

Every one of Prizeman's drawings has an air of illicit complicity about it. Alongside the ordinary folk, shady characters inhabit his world – second-hand car dealers, prostitutes. In his *Wolf Housing*, one group of towers had a park that bridged between them at roof level. This is no rooftop landscape such as at Le Corbusier's (1887–65) much-mimicked Unité d'Habitation in Marseilles (1947–52), but the domain of wolves that live happily but separately from the intense urban condos beneath them. In a typically obverse-perverse combination of Prizeman's, the presence of the wolves adds to the architectural and social attraction of the apartments below.

No wonder then that Diploma Unit 10's work that year turned out to be more of a challenge than the external examiners, architects James Stirling (1926–92) and Ed Jones (b 1939), were used to. Although silently viewing the work during the assessment procedure, it was not until the tutors and examiners gathered at the end of the day that they announced that to them, this work was un-assessable. As far as they could see, it was not architecture. What was to be done? In the end it was agreed that an alternative panel would look at the work, and thus the work was duly passed – but not without repercussions.

Building Design, 15 July
1983, front page.

News of the commotion
surrounding the final exams
of the AA's Unit 10 travelled
fast, and became the subject
of a scoop for BD. For
moderate offices up and
down the country, members
of Unit 10 represented a real
threat to the status quo.

A couple of days later *Building Design* had
the controversy as its cover scoop: 'AA STUDENTS IN
DESIGN ROW'.[6] Alvin Boyarsky (1928–90), the head
of the school, wanted us to prove that our skins had
been worth saving, so he offered us the opportunity
of publishing. He had a book in mind, but we soon
decided that a magazine would be a more vital
format, reaching more people more quickly.

The magazine needed a title – and
perhaps so did we as a group – so I suggested
to those gathered for our first meeting that both
should be called NATO: Narrative Architecture
Today. It captured the artistic mood of the time
and appropriated the treaty alliance for our own
purposes. Innocent enough, the name served us
well, and although relatively short lived, it led to
three issues of the magazine and a host of projects,
interjections and exhibitions over the following
three-year period.[7] *NATO1* appeared in the spring
of 1984.[8] As Rick Poynor said collectively of NATO,
'Its districts overlaid functions and meshed together
narratives in a provocative flux designed to cause
meanings to slip and reverse.'[9]

The group and the magazine provided a robust context in which,
like the Surrealists and their magazines, the imaginary could be treated as
a reality. At the time there was precious little opportunity for architects to
build. It is no exaggeration to say that the architectural scene was centred on
work produced by the schools and by architects who were practising with
their lifestyle rather than their designs. Apart from Cedric Price (1934–2003)
and Stirling himself, the commercial world of the prominent British firms of
Norman Foster (b 1935), Richard Rogers (b 1933), Ahrends, Burton & Koralek
and Nicholas Grimshaw (b 1939) seemed to us remote and irrelevant to the
future of the city.

We wanted to harness the turbulence that the huge social changes
of the time were causing. Our friends lived in squats and warehouses, with
beds inside greenhouses and on top of stacks of milk crates. People from all
creative fields, particularly from Saint Martins School of Art and the Royal
College of Art, were talking to each other and swapping ideas. NATO people
were more interested in artists, fashion folk and designers than in other
architects, as the pages of *NATO* magazine show. It was time to grasp the city

as a whole, along with everyone and everything in it, and the more chaotic the better. British architect Ralph Tubbs's (1912–96) observation from the war years, the 'crazy silhouettes of twisted steel', could be a slogan for the new post-war age that had come to pass years later.[10] A new war was being fought, breaking down the old hierarchies that even the liberated 1960s had not touched, and doing so by example as well as by design.

Thatcher delivered a fatal handbagging to the Greater London Council whose relentless crossfire from County Hall towards the Houses of Parliament had been an irritant to government. In 1984 I was invited by Boyarsky to make a solo show at the AA, and I decided on a project around the newly vacant County Hall as the site for a new Exhibition of Architecture that would stretch along the South Bank of the River Thames from St Thomas' Hospital to the Festival Hall, the only remaining part of the 1951 Festival of Britain.

The project took each of the principal sectors in this area of the South Bank and reworked them into an invading, flowing, marauding public territory that had the atmosphere of a building site, with its cranes, platforms and plastic bin chutes. It suggested both architecture and a society in a fervent state of flux. The resulting installation combined a variety of communication techniques, from a huge grungy model that spread out from the fireplace in the gallery to a colonnade of wiry stands on which hung a photographic storyboard of a TV news story with a 'reporter' (in photos) speaking from various locations soon to be transformed when the project went ahead. A set of six oil pastel drawings focused on each of the main conditions in the project, and a huge panelled 'painting' of the whole ensemble seen from the air occupied an entire wall.

Each one of the drawings in the set of six was a study of how existing buildings could be blown open, and could make way for an influx of new roofs, paths and people. The hermetic character of County Hall would in my version be subjected to the traffic flow that swirls around Waterloo Station. Dynamic business 'streets' would invade St Thomas' Hospital, County Hall and every building across the area. It would assume an exhibition-like up-scaling of reality by incorporating superhuman sculptures.

NATO1, 1983, magazine cover.

Soon after the exams debacle, NATO was formed as mouthpiece for the ideas of the Unit. A publication would help expound and explain. The group and the magazine had one and the same mission: to grab the freedom that a London in pieces had opened up.

NATO, 'Albionize Your Living Room', scan from *NATO2*, 1984.

Members of the group would egg each other on to produce more extravagant and brutish objects that could be used at home. Many were assembled into a single story that demonstrated how to do it yourself.

By 1984 the giant as a motif had appeared in various forms in NATO work. The first issue of the magazine featured *Albion*, the name given to the re-visioning of the South Bank at Bermondsey. The Roman giant Albion seemed an apt evocation of the new Britain, and since there are still numerous Albion Streets in the capital and countless more pubs by the same name, it was an idea that had resonance for many local people. The subsequent *ArkAlbion* had a Noah's Ark too, a lifeboat that was a metaphor for the lifesaving work of St Thomas'. Its slipway emerged from the hospital buildings and met the river surface amid a line of six giant fish tails. Effectively they made the river part of the exhibition.

As it appeared in *NATO2*, the 'Apprentice Issue', *ArkAlbion* captured a vision of the city as an endless building site.[11] Every construction in it was subject to functional reinterpretation. Conventional features of architecture such as the tower, the curtain wall and pilotis, gave way to signs of change, to scaffolding, tarpaulins and provisional contraptions of all kinds. The plastic bin chute was of particularly iconic importance. A fringe of them dangled like elephants' trunks from the facade of County Hall, and being as large as the columns they sprang out between, at least equalled the iconography of what had originally been built in Portland stone.

The NATO group – Martin Benson, Catrina Beevor, Peter Fleissig, Robert Mull, Christina Norton, Mark Prizeman, Melanie Sainsbury, Carlos Villanueva Brandt and myself – was acquiring the persona of a rock band,

and appeared in youth and lifestyle magazines including *L'Uomo Vogue* in Italy and *Brutus* in Japan. Magazines beget magazines, and one of our goals had come to be. It was possible to make a connection with the street style that was driving much of British youth culture. Rather than being confined to a discourse among architects, we managed to reach our target audience: people with a fashion, music or club sensibility as well as hungry young architects. The assumption that realised buildings would be the mainstay of architectural publishing was being called into question.

A degree of professional recognition was not that long in coming. The same year the 'Starchoice' exhibition at the RIBA in Portland Place, London, set out to bring several architects and designers together in a collaborative design venture. The star we chose was Derek Jarman, who by that time had become one of our favoured critics at the Architectural Association. He had a background in architectural history from his studies at King's College London,

Nigel Coates, model, 'ArkAlbion' exhibition, Architectural Association, London, England, 1984.

As Margaret Thatcher closed down London's government, this project visualised new uses for County Hall and the South Bank. An Exhibition of Architecture would invade the area with a dynamic exposé of urban processes. The distinctly anarchic flavour of the model is emphasised by its painted surfaces and artful wobble.

Nigel Coates, County Hall, 'ArkAlbion' exhibition.

With a bit of strategic demolition, County Hall could become a People's Palace for a new interactive sort of politics. Committees meet around mobile tables, while larger debates take place in open-air tribunes with powerful lighting. The looping public gallery encourages participants to keep on the move.

and despite his subsequent punk leanings towards radical clashes and vital instinct, he had a penchant for historicist whirls and twirls.

From a series of face-to-face encounters with Jarman, his dream house emerged from a transformed derelict building on the edge of a quarry on the Dorset coast above Dancing Ledge, a place that he had immortalised as the title of his first book. There was talk of a pet goat that would be tethered at the centre of the quarry, and the house itself would occupy the old stone structure midway between the quarry and the high cliff that plunges into the ocean. Despite the modesty of this structure, originally an engine room, the cross walls defined a series of spaces that could easily be assigned personable domestic functions. The largest of these would be an open-plan room with kitchen and sitting room, and the narrowest would become Jarman's library. Books would occupy a circular bookcase standing free from the structure, and topped with a 'pineapple' dome that would sprout from the roof.

From the outside, conventional walls would only exist as they had in the original ruined building. In turn we exaggerated these with giant scrolls set at incongruous angles, suggesting the presence of buried classical ruins. Sections of roof between these walls stretched down to the ground like giant tongues, and would be covered in grass, as if to hide the whole house and avoid attention from visitors to this well-known beauty spot.

Inside too the contrast between the over-scaled and singular modesty continued. A series of colossal legs acted as columns to support a mezzanine

ハイファイ・ライフの 未来風景

装置はいかにして都市生活に飲みこまれ、どろどろに消化されながら同時に見醒していくのだろうか。とりわけハードコアなテクノポリス、東京で未来のA&V生活を想像することは、不気味に刺激的である。ロンドン気鋭の建築家ナイジェル・コーツが描いてみせる我らがハイファイ・ライフの行く末、とくと御覧あれ。

walkway that, in turn, would lead to a narrow tunnel cutting through the rock, and emerging as a private 'balcony' looking out to sea. Lessons learnt here were many: this was a true collaboration, not only with Jarman, but involving most members of the group. It was a modest proposition that contrasted with the hyper-urban scale of most of our previous work, and yet, like the urban projects, it contained a potent theatricality that would be revealed over time.

　　　The whole NATO project reached an apotheosis with 'Gamma City', an exhibition first hosted in 1985 at Iwona Blazwick's brief but important AIR gallery in Rosebery Avenue, London. Subsequently it travelled to the Fruitmarket Gallery in Edinburgh (1986) and the Institute of Contemporary Art in Boston, Massachusetts (1987). Issue 3 of the magazine doubled up as the catalogue of the exhibition and the 'Gamma City Issue'. It proclaimed the deeply penetrating effect of gamma rays emanating from our architectural interventions. They would be transmitters of NATO dynamism over the rest of the city.

Nigel Coates, *Radical Technology*, 1984.

Drawing was an essential feature of NATO work, and the more furious the better. This imaginary apartment in Tokyo included several of my own devices such as the Footman television and the Wombat Wardrobe. The city outside appears to be a continuous building site.

Members of the NATO Group in their studio, photographed for *Brutus* magazine, 1987. (From left to right: Nigel Coates, Robert Mull, Mark Prizeman, Peter Fleissig and Carlos Villanueva Brandt.)

In the manner of a pop band, five NATO members are shown here at our studio in an old warehouse in London's Docklands before it was developed for yuppie housing. The pose, welding torch and vintage motorbike, emphasises our taste for heavy metal.

A simple phenomenological urban lexicon differentiated the two floors of the AIR Gallery: downstairs characterised the city as the Marketplace, while upstairs was the Boudoir. The show's ad-hoc spirit was announced predictably enough by a scaffolding addition to the building, and yellow plastic bin chutes poking from specially acquired tarpaulin sheets. Inside, a model swooped upwards as if to pass through the ceiling to the

NATO, Fast Forward: Tokyo 1997, published in *Brutus* magazine, 1987.

As part of this special issue of Brutus dedicated to creative London – which included the work of fashion designers, creative salvage folk, RCA graduates, and us as the architectural visionaries – NATO's future idea of Tokyo empathised its inherent chaos, fearless pluralism and obsession with experience-oriented technology.

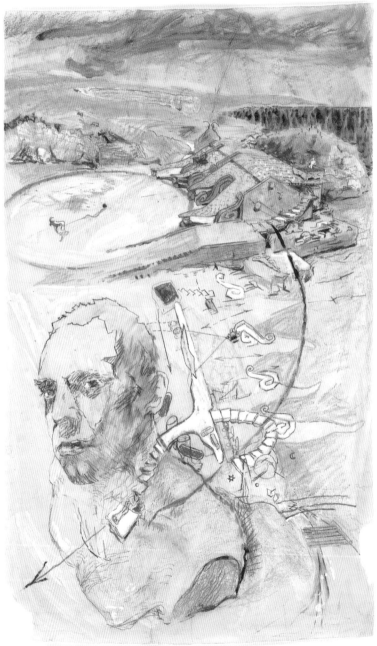

NATO/Nigel Coates, *Derek Jarman Ideal Home*, 'Starchoice' exhibition, RIBA, 1984: concept drawing.

Drawing as psychogeography: as if in Jarman's mind, the essentials of his dream house are laid out behind him. Giant scrolls exaggerate the old walls of a ruined structure in a picturesque Dorset quarry. Below, the internal circulation spine includes a spur that passes through the cliff to a lookout high above the waves.

NATO/Mark Prizeman,
Derek Jarman Ideal Home,
'Starchoice' exhibition,
RIBA, 1984: section.

Some of the more detailed
and perhaps contradictory
requirements are clearly
visible in this exuberant
section. The library occupies
a giant pineapple that bursts
through the roof, which on
the outside is disguised as a
knoll. The limbs of a colossus
support both an internal
walkway and the dining
table.

upper gallery, reinforcing the point that every activity of the city should reach
into others. As well as collecting some of the more iconic projects that had
been done over the previous years, new ones appeared, like Carlos Villanueva
Brandt's public baths sited in the Peabody Buildings opposite the gallery.
Catrina Beevor designed an office based on a garden, and Robert Mull made
a table so tall you could walk underneath it. My own Wombat Wardrobe
imported the vocabulary of the building site into the bedroom as a wardrobe
made from scaffolding and tarpaulins.

Models and furniture were an important addition to the architectural
show. There had been some furniture pieces made for the controversial AA
Unit show in 1983 (including two tables made from recycled car bonnets)
but in 'Gamma City' objects played a much more fundamental role. Three
collaged double-page spreads in NATO3 combined slogan, manifesto, object
and project. 'Gamma City' crossed an invisible boundary that differentiated
architecture from art. Without actually building the designs at full scale, both
magazine and exhibition brought the viewer into its own spatial framework.

At the AIR Gallery, we wanted a ricochet effect to fire between the
drawings, the real-scale objects and the actual and metaphoric scale of the
gallery. As objects and drawings bridged between disparate but otherwise

conventional fields, ambiguity was rife. Together the two floors of the show combined into one huge three-dimensional 'drawing' of the entire city. Likewise the magazine had stepped outside the conventions of the architectural project, and portrayed the reader as well as the building.

Post-NATO

Several years later, in 1992, some of these ideas translated into the 'Ecstacity' exhibition at the Architectural Association, a vision of central London overlaid with contrasting micro-narratives. Like 'Gamma City', this show attempted to combine real and represented space. Unlike it, the field of focus included not furniture but a frisson of mixed media. The show included a large print of a drawing I had done for *Vogue* magazine the previous year as part of a feature on what London might be like in 2066.

In my mind, by 2066 the city had become a field of cucumber-shaped towers with elevated motorcycle routes threading between them. Buckingham Palace had been handed over to the nation by King Charles as a new home for the Tate (then only housed at Millbank). The drawing showed the Thames, its banks housing a slew of new institutions in droopy structures. The general architectural mood was cyber-organic, with lots of rounded edges and plant-like constructions. Despite a strong sense that the city had evolved, demolition was not necessarily the order of things. In the future, buildings would be adapted in an ad-hoc manner. New construction would express a certain fluidity of mind. My impressionistic drawing technique leaned towards irregular naturalistic forms that hinted at movement instead of the decoration overload sported by most of London's well-known monuments.

The 'Ecstacity' idea was to aim for a city that expressed optimism and sensuality in its physical architecture. It would build on the fact that the new leisure-oriented city had (in my mind) become a huge success. Pleasure, it seemed, was the religion of the day, along with making money and spending it. Espresso coffee shops were popping up like champagne corks, and architecture practices with silly names were establishing themselves in Hoxton and Hackney. But there was also a new sensibility in the air; cyberspace

Cover of *NATO3* – 'Gamma City Issue', 1985.

NATO's largest ever exhibition took place at the AIR Gallery, a publicly funded art space in London. The third and final issue of *NATO* magazine doubled up as the catalogue for the show. The manifesto inside proposed a network of Gamma buildings that could transmit rays of creativity across the capital.

NATO's building regs, spread from *NATO3*, 1985.

Brian Hatton's 15 points exploited the format and language of building codes to rework NATO principles. It proved that architecture could be pared down enough to exist through text alone.

had entered the popular imagination with William Gibson's seminal novel *Neuromancer* which was published in 1984.[12]

From that same year, I spent considerable time in Tokyo and could see a neurological connection between the rushing experience of the city and the way my mind was working. By the early 1990s London was beginning to facilitate the mass hedonism that is now a permanent feature of city life. But it seemed to me that my body was also a laboratory for a new way of designing based on harnessing energy and using it as a tool for transformation. Could you treat the architecture – existing or imaginary – as though it were itself a body? Could you stroke it and tease it into a sensually responsive form?

It was the beginning of working with computers. In Branson Coates, my office at the time, we created an imaginary computer screen that, alongside the already familiar functions of cut, paste and copy, had invented functions like Ecstacise, Split, Shatter and Soften. With the help of the computer you could not only generate new shapes, but could take existing architecture and optimise it, as though a notional ecstasy pill had been administered to the physical environment of the city.

My approach to narrative was to extrapolate an imaginary flux that, while based in the present, would energise the speculative process of design. Rather than following the traditional critical appraisal of prevailing conditions and defining a brief through which to ensure improvement, I wanted to set the city free by empathising with what 'it wanted to be'. The vision certainly outstripped the tools available at the time, as the imagery clearly shows. Yet a methodology was forming, one that I did not completely understand. I was applying some of the raw enthusiasm of NATO days to the very heart of the city, with the confidence that even the icons of the state should respond to the optimism that was being reflected in smaller ways by the arty fashion culture that I and many others like me were living day to day.

The installation that housed all this used various devices to introduce the themes and then blow them up into a delirious rush of sweeping movement. A very large painting – 2.5m x 5m – stood against the long wall of the AA's gallery to explain the effects on the urban landscape of this new way of designing: cartoon-like representations of familiar London buildings

NATO, 'Beached', spread from *NATO3*, 1985.

The graphics crossed over with style and music magazines; NATO's raucous undercurrent is reflected in the clothing, the activity and the environmental snippets we had designed and built. A drawing of padded components and bendy structures anticipates the Boudoir, one of the central themes of the 'Gamma City' show.

NATO, 'Gamma City'
exhibition, AIR Gallery,
London, England, 1985.
On entering, the first exhibit
was a tabletop model of
central London with Gamma
buildings located at strategic
points across it. With
projects about the public
realm, the Marketplace
occupied the lower
exhibition floor. Upstairs the
Boudoir included plenty of
NATO furniture and project
ideas for the home.

like the National Gallery, the theatres along The Strand, the Adelphi, the
Savoy Hotel, the BBC at Bush House together with the bridges, the churches
and the northern embankment of the Thames.

Like earlier NATO drawings it had a sense of urgency, but this time
the image was painted. Alongside the familiar structures, new relatively alien
ones had been included. Huge paddle-like shapes hovered above existing
buildings and slipped, creature-like, into the river. Inverting expectations of
scale and temperament, an oversized benign figure reclined in the mass of
building that defines the curve of Aldwych. This was none other than the
giant Albion, asleep amongst the Portland Stone blocks that define most
institutional buildings in central London. I wanted the human figure to be
present at the size of the city itself – though not as a real proposition, more
as a pervasive, benign force of wellbeing.

The patterns for this large painted image had been created with a
quick visual technique using black ink and Japanese brushes on several layers
of tracing paper. Each layer was then projected onto canvas so it could be
painted in a predetermined colour, reproducing the detail in the brush sketch.

Nigel Coates, *London 2066*, 1991.

The text accompanying this drawing predicted: 'The City has become an agglomeration of shining steel towers of light jammed in among the nineteenth-century Florentine palaces that used to be banks ... Mediocre twentieth-century buildings have been replaced by *Neuromancer* medievalism. No longer a museum, the city is both living history and living future.'

Nigel Coates, Ecstacity computer program, 'Ecstacity' exhibition catalogue, Architectural Association, London, England, 1992.

Computer tools needed to up the Dionysian potential of existing cities. This hypothetical program could take the city as it stood and 'Ecstacise' it with tools like 'split' or 'shatter'. The screen is filled by four related windows; they frame design ingredients like 'Place', 'Use' and 'Narrative' that together equal the 'Situation'.

However the image was not completely without structure; I had devised a living map of generative planning, or 'pumplanning', for a whole raft of new identities for specific parts of the area sampled in the project. There was to be an annual art *fiera* on the north bank of the Thames housed in a series of shell-shaped pavilions. A pontoon called a 'zagramp' dipped into the river. Other features included 'iclones' and the 'memoring'. My architectural ideas sprang out with the words.

Concepts realised

At Branson Coates ways of working had evolved considerably since NATO days. The dynamic complexity of the group had developed into a more contained way of producing architecture like making a movie. Between the NATO period and 'Ecstacity', I had managed to put narrative architecture into practice. In projects such as Caffè Bongo in Tokyo (1985) and Katharine Hamnett's flagship fashion store in Knightsbridge, London (1987) (see chapter 5), I tried every technique going: from the filmmaker to the painter, from the scientist to the archaeologist, from the visionary to the designer-maker.

With the emerging speed of communications, both electronic and physical, the context of practice was changing beyond recognition. In order to make an architectural product you needed to understand that people had their own expectations of the urban environment. People outside the profession were not only taking an active interest in architecture and design, but also wanted to take the environment into their own hands. The arrival of the Internet facilitated shifting notions of community, with people being able to organise themselves more quickly and without hindrance into spaces that were not necessarily either made physically or by architects.

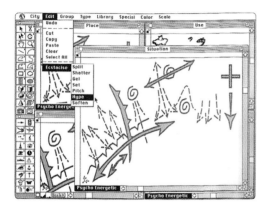

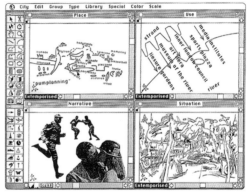

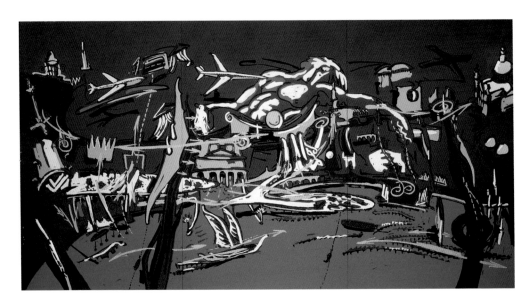

Yet architects continue to be in a unique position in terms of their potential to shape the environment and people's experience of it. Bars, clubs and clothing stores – places with an enhanced sense of drama and spectacle, and where awareness of identity, physicality and sexuality are often heightened – are particularly fertile ground for an engagement with narrative in architecture; but its relevance extends to all building types, and its very nature is diverse. My own enquiries have led me to identify three distinct narrative strands which can be used as a starting point for the creative process. These are presented in the next chapter, along with built work by innovators in the field that develops and exploits narrative in each of its various forms.

Nigel Coates, *Ecstacity* (painting), 1992.

This drawing was so large (2.5m x 5m) it had to be painted. It samples a central part of London between Trafalgar Square and Saint Paul's Cathedral. Ethereal new structures add a new energy to existing buildings. In the centre of the Aldwych crescent, the Giant Albion reclines as an artful reminder of the human psyche of the city.

References

1 Mary Banham and Bevis
Hillier, *A Tonic to the Nation:
The Festival of Britain 1951*,
Thames & Hudson (London),
1976.
2 Bernard Tschumi, *The
Discourse of Events*, exhibition
catalogue, Architectural
Association (London), 1983,
pp 94–5.
3 Tschumi, 'Spaces and Events',
ibid, pp 6–11.
4 Attila Kotányi, 'Gangland
and Philosophy', *Internationale
Situationniste*, No 4 (June

1960), pp 33–5.
5 Most of the work
mentioned appeared in the
NATO magazine, Issue 1,
Architectural Association
(London), 1983.
6 Leading article, *Building
Design*, 15 July 1983, p 1.
7 Brian Hatton laments that
NATO only produced three
issues in *The 80s: History
of Unit 10*, Architectural
Association (London), 2010.
8 *NATO* magazine, Issue 1,
Architectural Association

(London), 1983.
9 Rick Poynor, *Nigel Coates:
The City in Motion*, Fourth
Estate (London), 1989, p 36.
10 Ralph Tubbs, *Living in Cities*,
Penguin (Harmondsworth),
1942.
11 *NATO* magazine, Issue
2, Architectural Association
(London), 1984.
12 William Gibson,
Neuromancer, Gollancz
(London), 1984.

4

Story Buildings

'The medium is the message' is a phrase coined by Canadian philosopher
and educator Marshall McLuhan (1911–80) in his 1964 book *Understanding
Media*.[1] Extrapolating this construct into the present, narrative emerges as
a 'cool' medium. McLuhan describes the cinema as a 'hot' medium that
requires less effort on part of the viewer in assembling the details of a movie
image, yet the scrambled 'cool' stream of television requires more effort;
the more scrambled the medium, the greater the potential for spontaneous
interpretation.

   Although 20th-century Modernist architects would probably have
seen architecture as 'hot' in McLuhan's terms, I see it as 'cool' in that it
is both open to wide interpretation and requires effort on part of the
participant. The 'medium' of space is open and closed, multivalent and
transmutable. Architecture works by association, constantly mirroring and
differing from 'spaces' in the mind.[2] Like TV and the Internet, architecture
should hand the power of experience back to people.

   Around the year-2000 turning point, city environments have
successfully borne the weight of relentless marketing, neutralising the
aggressive 'overheated' messages (in the McLuhan sense) of advertising.
A cacophony of message-making levels out into a white noise of idealised
lifestyle options. Beauty, celebrity, rebellion, achievement and sexual prowess
each play their part in this highly tuned contemporary urban landscape.
We have learned to adapt to this Janus-like duplicity, and recognise the
extraordinary in the everyday and the everyday in the extraordinary.

Few architects would adhere to a structured design method, but one of the purposes of this book is to tease out some axiomatic manoeuvres. This chapter maps out a 'method' for using narrative as a design tool. Despite the risk of contradiction by some of the other designers I have chosen to highlight here, my aim in this chapter is to explore their designs in relation to these ideas.

Against the riches achieved by successive efforts of many hands, the work of the single architect seems parsimonious. Of course there are architects who are genuinely driven by simplicity itself. Peter Zumthor (b 1943) has built an elegant paradigm of the simple farmer's shed to house his studio in Haldenstein, Switzerland (1986). David Chipperfield (b 1953) demonstrates a masterful command of Rationalism in his City of Justice in Barcelona (2009) and at the Liangzhu Culture Museum, China (2007). Narrative layering comes through in the output of both, but as an after effect.

In this chapter I have identified built work that is driven by narrative; and by examining these projects I aim to reach a simple lexicon that distinguishes between three distinct forms of narrative genus: binary narrative, sequence narrative and biotopic narrative. Rather than simply carrying the imprint of archetypal memories, each of the following buildings draws the user into a complex psychological configuration. Some make simple combinations of function and metaphor; others incorporate a time dimension, either through a sequence drawn out in space, or as a matrix that presents an orchestrated variety of options.

Despite traces and afterimages, the basic mechanisms of narrative correspond to Kevin Lynch's elements of the city: path, edge, district, node and landmark.[3] All of these are subject to being propelled backwards or forwards in time, to a compression and expansion according to the possible effects of rhetorical emphasis. Seen as discrete, each element can be intensified with a narrative overlay. Orchestrated and at any scale – these spare parts of architecture are available for narrative conscription. Whether house, big building or mighty city, the rules are the same. The architect brings elements culled from the imagination into line with the rudimentary forms thought to be necessary to fulfil the task in hand.

Rather than Lynch's 'path', we could be looking at the circulation inside a building; rather than 'edge', we can talk about the wall, or the border of a carpet. Instead of 'district' think of rooms, 'nodes' as points of intersection like a hallway or the threshold between garden and terrace. And as for 'landmark', we may think of fireplace, television, a strategically positioned painting – even a computer. Landmarks need to mark a singular place axiomatically and uniquely to the user, even if the 'public space' is within the confines of the home.

We must now explore the concept of an architectural situation. Without resorting to the rather crude distinction between an interior and an exterior, a situation reduces a configuration of objects and enclosures

Will Alsop, The Big Frock, Toronto, Canada, 2005.

When asked to provide a working space for a sewing collective at the Toronto Design Fair, Alsop decided that a sartorial product would do the trick. Every visitor gets to explore the skirts in this simple but powerful coincidence of shelter and an out-of-scale object that normally would be the antithesis of architecture.

in space to a set of essentials. For example: the situation in your own living room might combine fireplace, the TV, your computer, a favourite chair with a light for reading, the enclosure around it and the doors and windows that puncture it. Perhaps there is a certain tree you see from the window, and a garden gate. This situation consists of all the components that are significant to the subject: you. Together they form a very personal geography, and one that can be adjusted slightly according to the moment. The chair can move, the fire be lit, etc, but the essential configuration stays the same, and forms a mental map. This sounds familiar enough and in a more archetypal form, this 'situation' is relevant as a model to apply to all houses. When thinking of entire buildings of any kind, their accommodation can be configured by a brief and a programme, but interpreting the task as a series of interrelated situations shifts the design process into manoeuvrable narrative territory.

Binary narrative

The first and the most straightforward kind of narrative has to be the 'binary'. This constitutes investing the object or 'situation' with a parallel identity – not one derived from function but trans-function – that is a function of the mind, a transgression, a sublimation, a presence from the imagination that can 'heat up' the otherwise banal object. Imagine you design a restaurant that celebrates, through the decor and the food, a faraway place otherwise disconnected from our own: an Indian restaurant with ogee arches around the windows and an interior column clad with metal leaves to look like a palm tree. Although this treatment might be an attempt to create an illusion, it also bears all of its contrivance without pretence. No one expects to be taken in, beyond the enjoyment of an atmosphere. It's a bit like having a bed in the shape of a Ferrari or a cocktail cabinet that looks like a Hawaiian hut.

Like art, it is very rare that a building pleases everyone; but many architects who try to do just that would do better to assume some of the bravado of the artist. Artists have sometimes taken on architecture with giant projections onto buildings, which became something of a fashion around the passing of the Millennium.

Will Alsop: The Big Frock, Toronto

Take, for example, the 2005 exhibition piece by Will Alsop (b 1947) that 'constructs' a workable space beneath the skirts of a giant dress. The organisers of a big interiors convention in Toronto asked Alsop to design a stand to promote the textile industry. They wanted a small space for machinists to work in, and at the same time to inspire visitors to the exhibition. A bit like a giant tea cosy, Alsop's design used the narrative of a voluptuous red dress to define an enclosure. The size and cut of the dress, the hooped structure inside it, the selection of the textile, and how the volume inside would work are all captured in one image that combines the context (the show), the use (machining) and the narrative (the dress). Because of the absence of a real female body, the structure would work entirely differently to a normal dress and, much enlarged, the fabric would need help in up-scaling the effect of folds and draping. Above all, the garment had to work as an icon within the show environment; it didn't have to 'fit' its surroundings in the normal sense of the word, but contrasted with them. Neither did it need to be a fashion statement. It had to be full of 'dressness', and be recognisable to everyone.

Alsop enjoys importing signs from other cultural fields and knocking architectural conventions into the bargain. As a fellow 'artist-architect', he takes a gamble on his own perceptions successfully transferring to his audience. His Chips apartment building in Manchester, completed in 2009, gives more than a nod to a very local food. He is designing on our behalf – and his. Like any confident designer, he needs to live and feel his materials and they just happen to include clothes, vehicles, body parts and cartoon characters. His scavenging amongst popular culture allows him to look for matches between forms and meanings that can be architecturalised, and occupied at the scale of buildings. His solutions undermine convention with narratives culled from popular culture, contaminating the familiar architectural vocabulary with an aesthetic that often borders on ugliness, yet compensates for it with very familiar 'roguish' signs.

As the design process first sites and then converts the chosen narrative, it creates a rhetorical trope that can be applied spatially and architecturally. A trope is a figurative illustration, exaggerated to suit the purpose. Alsop's dress is any dress, a type, and in the conversion from idea to reality adapts to need, but becomes the trope of the dress, its sign. This postmodern process approximates to Victorian high camp, like London's Albert Memorial (George Gilbert Scott, 1863–72) and its partner opposite, the Royal Albert Hall (Francis Fowkes, 1867–71), and numerous town halls, banks and office chambers all over Britain. These assemblages of multiple 'tropes' drew from European buildings still fashionable to latecomers on the Grand Tour – a roof from here, windows from there, pilasters from somewhere else. Italian Gothic would happily be mixed with English Gothic, and without irony, a spire would poke freely upwards from a church based on a Greek temple. These architectural quotations would be used to tame any newly conceived institutional function, like a museum, a hospital, a workhouse – in fact just about any Victorian institution.

SITE: Best supermarkets, USA

SITE, BEST Inside/Outside Building, Milwaukee, Wisconsin, USA, 1984.

One of Site's many versions of the supermarket in reverse; the typically straightforward double signifier of the binary narrative in which the commercial shed is both asserted and undermined. A witty statement on the lack of substance of out of town stores, the ruined wall falls away to reveal the familiar serviced glass box behind it.

In the late-1970s' USA, a similar strategy of contrived brutalism was being applied to the supermarket chain Best. James Wines, an architect who had picked up on conceptual art, could see the potential of applying some of its honed irony to improve the commercial shed already familiar in most American suburbs. His idea was simple and effective: that the box be subverted by a variety of interventions – the peeling surface, the collapsed wall, the bombed-out building. A distinct intervention would give identity to each location while maintaining the identity of the brand. These narrative gestures, carried out between 1970 and 1984, were not that different from the cartoon customising that adorned many highway businesses, like doughnut shops in the shape of their own freshly baked product. Where they were different was in their adherence to the physical substance of the building. The parent structure was fused with Wines's intervention. Perhaps

at first people would ask if something tragic had befallen their favourite supermarket. They were witty, even funny in their implausibility, and proved effective enough for the formula to be repeated across the chain.

Herzog & de Meuron with artist Ai Weiwei: Beijing National Stadium, Beijing

When China won the bid to host the Olympics in 2008, it was an opportunity for the country to demonstrate its internationalism, modernity and fairness as expressed through the various building types necessary to house the various events. By now the Olympic Stadium by Herzog & de Meuron has become a postcard building that rivals the Eiffel Tower and Tower Bridge as a sign of unity and cooperation. Known as 'the Bird's Nest', the building itself is so nest-like as to comply with a powerful binary narrative. Though less ironic than the popular naming of Norman Foster's Swiss Re building in London (2001–3) as 'the Gherkin', its appellation is well accepted. Although the irregular horizontals of the outer framework related to Herzog & de Meuron's experimental trajectory of textures and facades since their inception as a practice, the forming of this open lattice into structure and circulation reinforces the inherently nest-like 'situation' of the inside of the stadium. To date it is the most figurative of the practice's works, and a powerful one at that.

Diller Scofidio: Blur Building, Swiss National Expo 2002

It seems that expo sites, which need powerful accessible statements, are well suited to the binary narrative. At the Swiss National Expo that took place in

Herzog & de Meuron, Olympic Stadium, Beijing, China, 2008.

The erratic exterior structure exaggerates scale, making it bigger (colossal) and smaller (birdlike) simultaneously; the nest wraps and disguises the stadium inside so that this narrative completely camouflages the actual function to become an icon in its own right.

The star turn at the Swiss
Expo, this 'fountain' puts
an offshore platform to
inventive use; it converts
lake water into a cloud
that responds to local
weather conditions such as
barometric pressure, wind,
temperature and humidity.
Visitors dressed in plastic
tourist macs would enter and
literally disappear into the
ever-changing cloud.

four locations around the shores of Lake Neuchâtel in 2002, Diller Scofidio
designed 'Blur', one of the most accomplished expo buildings ever. Using
water from the lake, their idea was to create an artificial weather system
that would respond to the prevailing conditions of temperature, wind and
atmospheric pressure.

Structure, image and story were fused such that the cloud narrative
and the technology that permitted it combined into one planetary entity.
Visitors wearing protective plastic waterproofs would enter its structure and
'disappear' into the artificial cloud that hovered in and around the open
structure. As it appeared to the public, this was not so much a building
as a natural phenomenon captured, like a kite being held on an unusually
short tether. Even though there were no walls as such, the building was
absolutely architectural (it was dismantled the following year). It had space
and substance, corridors, stairs and platforms that, when experienced from
within, gave the impression of being inside this living cloud.

AOC: No 1 Lower Carbon Drive, London

To showcase a Green Guide to Eco-products, the AOC (Agents Of Change)
came up with No 1 Lower Carbon Drive (2007), a mock-up of a conventional
terraced house situated in London's Trafalgar Square. Although not strictly

energy conserving in its own right, the open slice through the terrace was intended to reveal the anatomy of a house, including the services as well as the stairs and rooms themselves. Its narrative lies in the adaptation of the house as a well-understood typology that was then used as a mannequin for introducing new ways to save energy in your home.

FAT: Roadworks, London and Grote Koppel, Amersfoort

With Roadworks (1996), one of the most successful and visible urban art projects of the group FAT (Fashion Architecture Taste), several artists (including myself) were invited to 'transform' one of the bus shelters in the southern parts of the London Borough of Camden. The most effective

The AOC, No 1 Lower Carbon Drive, London, England, 2007.

Real-life as narrative: a stripped-back but resonantly ordinary house becomes special because in its new location, its banality turns into base typology of urban life in England. Visitors experience the guilt-inducing lower-carbon model in contrast with the shockingly wasteful reality of their own home.

Beaconsfield Artworks, thatched bus shelter, part of 'Roadworks', curated by FAT, London, England, 1996.

One of a series of altered bus shelters, this thatched version overturns the usual industrial Adshel version. Its overtly traditional technique not only renders it precious and handmade, but also suggests a cottage in a countryside context far from the pressures of the Tottenham Court Road.

FAT, Grote Koppel restaurant and office building, Amersfoort, The Netherlands, 2010.

This small commercial development made the most of its historic setting, not by fitting in, but by reinterpreting its surroundings as pattern and decoration. A series of typical cut-out facade details echoes the Dutch Renaissance vocabulary of nearby houses.

solution was the simplest – a thatched roof on an otherwise normal Adshel. For FAT and friends, Surrealist technique seemed to be alive and well. The only difference was that true Surrealists Man Ray (1890–1976) and André Breton (1896–1966) rarely managed to intervene in the street itself, preferring to treat it as a resource rather than a site.

Whether nearer to montage or *bricolage*, these examples diverge from the determinism of the Modernist architectural method, and introduce artistic imagination as a narrative component. If you were to approach an architectural design problem from this position, and played up - indeed exaggerated - the need to 'fit' within existing surroundings, you would be designing according to narrative principles.

Much later in Amersfoort, Holland, a local entrepreneur commissioned FAT to celebrate the foundation of the city some 750 years before with the Grote Koppel building (2010). Being adjacent to one of the city gates and a row of 19th-century warehouses, the site demands a contextual response with a twist. In Holland the classical merchant's house has a facade with a resonant flatness, which FAT have taken up in their merging of several cut-out layers into a single facade that wraps around the building. Inside is a restaurant with some offices upstairs, but the outside has a layered referential narrative reproducing the frontages of other buildings in the town. These are reduced to the size of the windows, so that as well as keying into the language of the warehouse, it also contains the facades of whole streets scaled down to a single floor.

Enric Miralles, Santa
Caterina Market,
Barcelona, Spain, 2005:
interior. (Opposite)
Inside the market it's
business as usual, but now
the experience assumes a
fervent modernity with more
than a nod to Gaudí.

Enric Miralles, exterior of
Santa Caterina Market.
In an exact exercise in
re-clothing the original
structure, Miralles both
floats a wavy-tiled surface
above the existing, and ties
it down with an elaborate
system of giant steel guy
ropes.

Enric Miralles: Santa Caterina Market, Barcelona

On a much larger, pointedly democratic scale, Enric Miralles's (1955–2000)
Santa Caterina Market (2005) in the historic centre of Barcelona took its
narrative from the city itself. Its voluptuous vaults and brightly coloured
tiles hover acrobatically above the perimeter of the original market building.
Rather like the canopies that protect archaeological excavations, this roof
springs from foundations shared with the original. Adopting a plant-like
tendency to grow slightly skewed, the new roof picks up on many of the
traditional qualities of covered markets, yet completely reinterprets them:
massive irregularly structured beams enable great spans of uninterrupted
space that accommodate the changing needs of the food stalls inside. Slatted
grills above the entranceways fill in the Gaudíesque trajectories formed by
the vaults as they project beyond the original host structure. The alchemical
combination of the waving roof and the more conventionally rooted structure
combines as a clear yet hyper-dynamic binary narrative. The two components
– the recuperated original and the new roof – do not so much merge as
coexist in a state of suspended coital intensity.

Sequence narrative

Although most art museums allow the visitor to flow relatively freely from room to room, curators of most temporary exhibitions want to tell a story in a structured way. They want to guide the viewer from space to space, whether indicating progress chronologically or a chain of ideas. This articulation is of the 'sequence' kind that lays out spaces along a predetermined route tying together several 'situations', each of which has its own spatial coherence.

Although not always sequential, English landscape gardens were designed to stimulate a sense of reverie by materialising mythical events and places, like Roman cascades or Greek temples, such as at Rousham in Oxfordshire (see chapter 1). A visit would take you along a prescribed route, in which each of the scenarios was distanced from the others so as not to contaminate one with another. There are numerous ways in which sequences unfold in urban environments, the most obvious being the roadway itself, and the routes that we choose to make in our endeavours to cross the town.

Driving, you surrender to the satnav as it leads you through a variety of junctions and turnings, many of which may seem to be completely incongruous and to contradict your own knowledge of the city. Avoiding formalised evidence, the contemporary *dériviste*'s freedom does not visibly mark the city – but then neither does a bus route on which, as a passenger, you could enjoy taking the journey for the journey's sake. A ghost train at the fair or a ride at Disneyland controls this sequencing further. Visitors queue up to be fed into the experience machine and are led blindly along rails or canals which focus their attention on contrasting scenes that, when assembled in the mind, add up to an entertaining experience.

Visitor attractions tend to have their own sophisticated internal logic that economises on the volume and means to deliver the magic. If you were to cut a section through Disneyland's 'Pirates of the Caribbean' or 'Big Thunder Mountain' rides, all the gubbins would be revealed: belts, chutes, cabling, ducting and pistons that feed the 'lifelike' experience for the punters up above.

Airports are slightly more functional versions of these attractions. Even though they gather and fan out passengers towards their gates, essentially airports are built around sequence organisation restricted to two cross-movements: those generated by departures and arrivals. Security and passport control constitute specific 'situations' along the routes back and forth between landside and airside; their linearity elaborates plot-wise into a variety of distractions in the form of shops and cafés, each with their own sub-narratives.

Lina Bo Bardi: SESC Pompéia, São Paulo

The SESC Pompéia (1977–82) in São Paulo offers a more benign and less
commercially optimised sequence narrative; it exists to encourage and
entertain, so its spatial organisation is more to do with the user than the
mechanics of a port.

For many people São Paulo can be an aggressive and difficult
place to live. Its sheer scale and complexity belie innumerable seemingly
disconnected valleys, each large enough to be a city in itself. Some are

Lina Bo Bardi, SESC Leisure
Centre, Pompéia, São
Paulo, Brazil, 1977–82:
beach.

Situated in a defunct
industrial complex, Bo Bardi's
first community leisure
centre retains its origins
as a narrative. Connecting
internal 'streets' draw visitors
through a variety of leisure
options including an artificial
beach. Every signifier
has a double: one utterly
functional and one pure
fantasy, as confirmed by the
painted jungle as a backdrop
to the sundeck boardwalk.

Lina Bo Bardi, SESC Leisure Centre, Pompéia, São Paulo, Brazil, 1977–82: workshop.

Many of the interior spaces have an exaggerated functionality to the point where they seem provisional. Caged storage units in the ceramics studios are built of breeze blocks but retain a sense of artistry with their curved layout.

valleys of the rich, but most are of the poor. In one of the most run-down parts of the city, Lina Bo Bardi (1914–92) made it her place to level some of this social inequality by building a community centre, the SESC Pompéia. The project undertook the conversion of an existing factory complex into a multi-purpose building that houses theatres, gymnasiums, a swimming pool, bars, leisure areas, restaurants, galleries, workshops and, most strangely of all, an artificial beach.

From São Paulo the sea is unreachable for the majority, so to include the seaside in the project would touch a nerve for many people. In sympathy with SESC's original industrial buildings, their conversion celebrates basic construction materials, and applies them to robust forms with workaday directness. You approach the boardwalk from the main entrance to the complex along an avenue between the converted sheds that house the theatre, library and workshops. This street ends abruptly as it hits the boardwalk laterally. At this juncture, visitors come face to face with a giant mural of the jungle complete with birds and animals. Of course it's an illusion, and just one component of an elaborate narrative mixing signs and activities that unfolds as you explore the boardwalk 'beach'. Needless to say this beach is heavily used, and disbelief suspended. Sunbathing here, *paulistanos* can perhaps forget that they are in the thick of one of the largest and most polluted cities in the world.[4]

Diller Scofidio + Renfro: The High Line, New York City

The High Line (2009) in New York is a further example of nature being hauled back into the urban environment. After years of neglect, Diller Scofidio + Renfro completed the project to reclaim this elevated railway, and orchestrate an overlapping of nature with this piece of industrial archaeology in the heart of the city. Stretching from the Meatpacking District in the south to Hudson rail yards in Midtown Manhattan, the park has a musical variation of tone and temperament. Benches rise from rail-like elongated tiles that alternate with untamed vegetation, as if the grass had been combed through rather than cut. Paths switch from one side to the other, and rise up to make a place to sit; stairs and ramps dip down to the street below. According to the architects, this is 'agri-tecture', and plainly a public space in which nature and landscape substantiate an elaborate sequence narrative that runs right through the heart of the city, and yet is lifted free from it. Kevin Lynch again:

> There is a (final) way of organizing a path or a set of paths, which will become increasingly important in a world of great distances and high speeds. It might be called the "melodic" in analogy to music. The events and characteristics along the path – landmarks, space changes, dynamic sensations – might be organized as a melodic line, perceived and imaged as a form which is experienced over a substantial time interval ... The form might be the classical introduction–development–climax–conclusion sequence, or it might take more subtle shapes, such as those which avoid final conclusions.[5]

Diller Scofidio + Renfro, The High Line Park, New York, USA, 2009-11.

For years the rotting hulk of the West Side railway had little to offer apart from industrial archaeology, but now it is light enough to make a child out of every visitor. Paving based on the erstwhile sleepers twists and turns into occasional groups of benches and sun loungers.

Olafur Eliasson, *The Weather Project*, The Turbine Hall, Tate Modern, 16 October 2003 to 21 March 2004.

The former Bankside Power Station provides the narrative basis for Herzog & de Meuron's much praised conversion. Shown here is Eliasson's *The Weather Project* (2003), the fourth in a series of annual commissions for the monumental Turbine Hall space. This economic but powerful installation succeeded in transcending any normal experience of an interior.

Herzog & de Meuron: Tate Modern, London

The Tate's competition to transform the old Bankside Power Station was won with a relatively sober project by Herzog & de Meuron. The resulting museum of contemporary art is inconclusive (and therefore embraces change) precisely because its narrative operates in reverse perspective: its existing buildings continue to supply a narrative with an open-ended effect that transgresses any sense of completion.

Tate Modern opened its doors to the public in 2000, and has been a resounding success ever since. The architects successfully overcame the limitations of confined fenestration with artificially lit galleries, and dramatic effects of height and volume with escalators that bypass intermediary floors to speed the public to the principal galleries on levels 3 and 5. Although the original building is symmetrical, with the chimney in the centre of the river facade, the adaptation to its gallery function stems from the ramp that cuts dramatically into the Turbine Hall at basement level from one end of the building. This sets up a sequence path that cuts across the symmetry of the whole, and with escalators that zigzag up through its various gallery levels.

As visitors descend the ramp, they gradually become aware of the enormity and particularity of the Turbine Hall, qualities that have been exploited to great effect by a programme of installations – including Olafur Eliasson's *The Weather Project* (2003) – that have responded to the unusual scale of the space. By occupying a rejected building of such innate yet obsolete power, a found object has provided a narrative that heightens an awareness of its present function as a gallery.

Rem Koolhaas/OMA: Prada Store, New York City

The descending ramp also comes into play at Rem Koolhaas's 2003 re-conversion of a large warehouse space on Broadway for the fashion brand Prada. In the 1990s the building had been the Guggenheim Museum's

Rem Koolhaas, Prada store, New York, USA, 2001.

The stock simplicity of the New York loft has literally been undermined to convert it into a fashion store-cum-museum. Visitors enter an installation that exaggerates every stage in the experience; the central section of the store is excavated into a theatrical pit. Identical retro mannequins occupy the steps to face the visitor. Merchandise hides in a series of underground spaces.

downtown space, and the gallery atmosphere was to be carried over into its new guise as a shop. Koolhaas had become fascinated by fashion as a metaphor for the times, and in turn Miuccia Prada was fascinated with Koolhaas's irreverent and mind-bending approach to common architectural problems such as shop design. He wanted to make the SoHo store into a performance space, where at first the clothes would play an unusually minor role. The product was discreetly confined to a relatively small area in the laundry level below ground, with most of the upper floor being carved away to make a large indoor public space. The narrative here revolves around the brand itself that at the time was being positioned as culture as much as fashion. The narrative was Koolhaas himself on a cultural catwalk that exhibits his interests in modern China, fashion as performance and the dynamics of consumer society.

Amanda Levete Architects (AL_A): New Exhibition Road entrance, Victoria & Albert Museum, London

Rem Koolhaas, Prada store, New York, USA, 2001.

The rhetorical elaboration continues on the rails; hanging screens displaying consumer artefacts render the clothes themselves artworks.

To complete this brief exploration of sequence narrative, I have chosen another project that takes its cues from existing buildings. The ambitious repaving of Exhibition Road as the public space that links the principal museums in South Kensington has led the V&A to upgrade the entrance behind the Aston Webb (1849–1930) screen on its western facade. A similar attempt had been made with the ill-fated Spiral designed in 1996 by Daniel Libeskind (b 1946), but this time, instead of making a shrill anti-contextual statement, Levete's 2011 proposal is relatively modest, and 'sinks in' to the existing courtyard. It will hardly be seen at all from the street.

A large new temporary exhibitions gallery will be created 12 metres below street level, so the design concentrates on how to ease visitors downwards in a calm and engaging experience peppered with unexpected views. From the street, what was previously a blind courtyard will be visible through a cleaned-up version of the original stone screen. This opens out into what Levete calls a 'public living room' that is split over two levels that allow views into the adjacent ground-floor galleries.

Almost incidentally, a canopy in the northeast corner indicates a café and, beyond that, access to the new gallery below via a wide zigzagging staircase. The surface treatment of the courtyard suggests geological strata; the front and rear areas seem to have shifted as a result of some seismic activity below, creating various openings in the ground that allow contact with the gallery beneath, both visually and by the stairs. Although not an enfilade in the traditional sense, the scheme makes use of a temporal sequence with various degrees of permanence, from ancient rock formations to the latest temporary exhibition. Along the way, visitors are treated to subtle flashbacks and forward glimpses.

Biotopic narrative

Speaking of the qualities to strive for in city design, Kevin Lynch said: 'The form must be somewhat noncommittal, plastic to the purposes and

AL_A, V&A Exhibition Road, London, 2011: new gallery space.
Like many of the marble floors within the museum, Levete's clean flowing white surfaces fit well within the eclectic vocabulary of the V&A's existing buildings. Splits and folds draw together the complex levels that surround this public 'living room'.

perceptions of its citizens.'[6] This led naturally to the desired effect of biotopic narrative. A biotope ('bio' together with *topos*, Greek for 'place') is a small, uniform environment occupied by a community of organisms, such as the bark of a tree that is home for several kinds of organisms – say lichen, fungi and insects – in a mutually beneficial micro-world.

In architecture, 'biotope' suggests an urban field that includes a variety of functions and storylines that are mutually supporting yet independent, as on a university campus or in an urban village. In the context of narrative, it captures an interrelated set of conditions with their own internal influences and dynamics. A field under study becomes a biotopic narrative when a system of narrative components fuses with its system of functional parts, like the occasional sparks between two electrically charged planes. It can destabilise the physical reality of a territory, therefore allowing it to be open to multiple interpretations. Itself a paradigm of the urban condition, it defines a territory of many 'situations' wired up nodally into a coherent network. With no need for formal organising devices, a biotopic narrative helps create a homogeneous condition of equal opportunities; it simultaneously exhibits functional clarity and stimulating incongruity, form and fiction.

To be in this landscape is to be aware of two worlds at once, in which each migrates towards the other. Whether visitor or inhabitant, frequent user or tourist, the subject senses a lift on physical surroundings,

AL_A, V&A Exhibition Road, London, 2011: view of courtyard at night.

As you emerge from the zigzag stairway, geological references transform into a sweeping Nervi-esque roof. Natural light filters into this new exhibition space and, in doing so, subliminally reinforces the presence of the courtyard above.

a certain volatility that puts experience before any verifiable reality. Architecture, the city and the not city can join in an open-ended system of meaning constructed by users making their own connections. A military encampment has something of these qualities, as does a department store, a fairground or a university campus.

At times an entire city can have this sense of a resounding double existence; to live in it is to lock on to its frequency. Such is the city for subsections of society – the many minority groups and modern tribes – that invent their own secret and largely invisible urban codes that can be read discreetly without fear of reprisal. Speaking of the fragility of Berlin, architectural commentator Francesca Ferguson writes: 'With the rise in small-scale architectural and design practices, design and film production outfits, a significant black market economy accounting for over 15% of Berlin's GDP, and a burgeoning immigrant population, the city could be regarded as more of a border city; a base for micro-production networks; and a self-organised autonomous subsystem.'[7]

This reality suggests quite different ways of shifting the ecology of cities with tangible alternatives to conventional planning. 'In the realm of alternative economies, this focus on a fragmented urbanisation could make way for a more useful "reading" of the city, one that could be harnessed even further as a micro-political tool, one that is ultimately able to impact upon conventional urban planning processes.'[8] Just as avant-garde fashion culture of the 1980s has been absorbed into mainstream communication techniques, the fallout from the collapsed global banking system is likely to shift the ecology of cities towards a responsive networked economy. Maybe there will even be pop-up banks.

Carsten Höller: The Double Club, London

The artist Carsten Höller (b 1961) collaborated with Prada and restaurateur Mourad Mazouz to make The Double Club (2008), an art installation and temporary restaurant in the North London borough of Islington that combined Congolese and Western culture. A literal crossover, two autonomous and entirely distinct rooms had been dovetailed into one. Giant slices divided the rooms like a cake, with cultural tropes emphasising the differences between the two. The two sources behaved as narratives for each other, and while not straying from their prescribed territory, had the bizarre effect of not reflecting, of illustrating by ignoring the effects of the other. That same year Höller installed giant slides in the Turbine Hall at Tate Modern, undermining the temple-like atmosphere of the gallery with a ludic

Carsten Höller and Fondazione Prada, The Double Club, Islington, London, England, 2008: Two Horse Riders Club.

In collaboration with restaurateur Mourad Mazouz, Höller has spliced together two radically different environments as if two cakes had been combined in one. Congolese and Western worlds cross into one another and cannot be separately occupied, so visitors cannot help crossing territories.

Carsten Höller and Fondazione Prada, Tile Garden Krutikow at The Double Club.

In an ironic characterisation of Western desires to achieve Utopia, Höller's wall tiles image a future in which people live in floating cities. Rendered in traditional blue ceramic, their combination of impossibility and overt banality perfectly captures the narrative sensibility.

intervention that exploits the disproportionate height of the space. Whether the slides or The Double Club, Höller's interest is in contradictory yet equally powerful doubles that put the observer in a position of having to draw the two together. Here his method keeps the two simultaneously visible but artificially separated by an invisible prophylactic barrier.

Rei Kawakubo et al: Dover Street Market, London

Freeform invasion is more the metre adopted by one of the most acutely fashionable emporia in the world, Dover Street Market (2005) on the Mayfair street of the same name. A global system of cultural tides provides one of the overriding narratives that extend way beyond fashion into politics, art and ideas. Dover Street Market perfectly captures this artful internationalism. Five floors of what was a dull office building backing on to Bond Street have been turned into a recycled version of the old Kensington Market – a hippie enclave where, in its heyday in the mid-1970s, you could buy everything from brothel creepers to loon pants. Dover Street, however, is an emporium for the rich and stylish. Although it plays on the makeshift style of 1970s' precedent, the scaffolding and chipboard, the taxidermy and garden sheds, create a scenery that does not purport to function beyond the fact that it provides a setting for the clothes and hiding places for the tills.

Rei Kawakubo et al, Dover Street Market, London, England, 2005.

In a conscious reworking of the erstwhile Kensington Market, Comme des Garçons fuses high-priced garments and accessories in an allotment aesthetic. Cash desks are in sheds casually placed to counter the logic of the building. Using a variety of cheap and temporary construction, each of the five floors tries to outdo the others.

NL Architects: BasketBar, Utrecht

Dwarfed but not outshone by much larger constructions at the OMA-
masterplanned campus at Utrecht University, NL Architects' BasketBar (2003)
is a spirited extramural confection of bars, lounges and a games court. It
sports a big cage for basketball on top, oversized in comparison with the
crush bar beneath it, which is partly sunk into the ground. This clever and
spirited layer-cake lays functions on top of one another, and allows the
curvaceous orange lounge to ooze out from the side. It complies with the
biotopic narrative model because of the formal, aesthetic and compositional
dynamics the design achieves with its three distinct parts.

     First the objects: the basket court is taller and wider than the glass
box housing the bar which is sunken to waist height, like a swimming pool.
From outside you enter along the bar top, which is at street level, and then
step down into the bar itself. Look upwards, and you see a large circular
rooflight that marks the centre of the games court overhead. While playing

basketball, you'd be pacing back and forth across this same glass circle; in between athletic bursts you catch glimpses of your friends enjoying a pint. A stairway on the side of the structure links it to the crazy-golf-shaped sunken terrace incorporating a long curving banquette and a ramp for disabled access. This is not so much cross programming as free planning, an amalgam of three components cleverly interlinking, with each penetrating the other with little 'situations'. Despite each of the objects possessing objective clarity, combined they build a biotopic narrative out of relative behaviours: each of the 'actions' informs and invades the others.

Enric Miralles: Scottish Parliament, Edinburgh and Parc Diagonal Mar, Barcelona

Enric Miralles proved to be one of the most natural exponents of narrative. He translated gesture and emotion into physical form with the ease of a calligrapher's brush. Like Santa Caterina Market and the Parc Diagonal Mar (1997–2000) in Barcelona, his Scottish Parliament (1998–2002) is a Wonderland of interlocking puzzle pieces, leaf and boat shapes built around the activities of parliament. This complex layered and swirling plan includes the debating chamber, a building for members' offices, four committee towers, and a listed 17th-century house. Miralles's design draws inspiration from the swelling landscape of Arthur's Seat, the historical palimpsest of the Royal Mile and the craggy pile of Holyrood Palace. He derives decorative detail by framing situations, like the thinking balconies that project from the facade of the members' building. The cliff-like exterior is frequently punched with crevices and nesting ledges. In the undercroft enclosing the entrance lobby one senses the displaced volume of the debating chamber above, itself a series of upturned hulls of Viking ships. The encrusting meaning is so dense that the ornate High Victorian Natural History Museum in London (Alfred Waterhouse, 1870–80) seems austere by comparison.

At the coastal end of the palm-lined Avenida Diagonal, the Parc Diagonal Mar occupies a large open rectangle between speculative housing blocks. The park was completed in 2002, two years after Miralles died. But all his ludic strategies are in evidence; just as in his reading of the Scottish landscape, the design draws forth, twists and exaggerates the larger surroundings of Barcelona, and mixes these with a witty interpretation of nature like the artificial lake with reed-bed shores. Towards the northern end, conventional planting gives way to whipping vines of steel that outsize nature, and contextualise the visitor in an Alice-in-Wonderland surrealist playground. Giant vases suspended amongst the vines refresh the Gaudí

NL Architects, BasketBar, University of Utrecht, Holland, 2003.

In contrast with the heavy buildings that surround it, this combined basketball court and bar bring a lightness to students' off time. Visitors to the bar enter along the bar itself; when seated they catch glimpses of the game above them through an oculus that marks the centre of the court.

tradition. This is a magical world with as much movement as Capoeira, turning a flat land into a rich and animated artificial landscape, and rendering the hopes of Japanese architect Kazuyo Sejima (b 1956) an understatement: 'In an age of non-physical communication by various means, it is the job of

Enric Miralles, Scottish Parliament, Edinburgh, Scotland, 1998–2002: exterior.
In an attempt to reflect the history and complexity of Scottish culture, this rich corpus refers to the sea, mountains and to the tenacious Scottish character. With its complex views and walkways, the public space in front of the building provides a rehearsal for the inside.

Enric Miralles, Interior of Scottish Parliament.
The chamber floats beneath a timber hull, while members' private rooms project seats 'in conversation' onto a cliff-like facade. This building refuses to relax; it draws the visitor into its network of narrative fragments at every opportunity.

Enric Miralles, Parc Diagonal Mar, Barcelona, Spain, 1997–2000.

Reactivating the Gaudí tradition, this exuberant park successfully offsets the banal housing blocks that surround it. A marsh lake dominates one end and a Wonderland rose garden the other. Whipping loops of steel support giant vases covered in smashed ceramics. These ludic devices assert fantasy as opposed to the eco-complexity of nature.

the architect to provide real spaces for communication between people.'[9] Miralles delivered people-space in spades.

Jean Nouvel: Serpentine Gallery Pavilion, London

Designed by Jean Nouvel (b 1945), the 2010 Serpentine Gallery Pavilion satisfies the need for a meeting place in the park with an oversized version of television's Big Brother House realised entirely in red. The narrative appears to be derived from the leisurely mood of the park, and the pluralistic activities that it contains.

Sitting on the green in front of the gallery building, its collection of deliberately dumb planar components has the air of a Scout encampment. Canopies fixed to elevated beams can be extended diagonally like the flysheets of tents to provide protection from rain or sun. Their loose composition allows lots of cross-penetration with the trees and grassland around it; yet the violence of the red balances out the benign force of nature, and, in doing so, draws together the sense of occupancy of a building and the freedom associated with boundless landscapes. In this open framework, Nouvel lays out some competing activities. A centrally located bar services

visitors, whether they are seated in the gazebos that define one edge of the pavilion, or are taking a break from a table tennis match.

Gianni Pettena: Family House, Isle of Elba, Italy

Gianni Pettena has been building his house on the Isle of Elba since in 1975 he bought an overgrown plot of land edged by cliffs, and looking out to sea. The project started with a 2m x 2m block with bunk beds on one side and a WC and sink on the other. Since then the house has grown organically, but not by extending the original modest structure. Pettena decided to split the notion of the house apart, with bedrooms and sitting rooms deliberately distanced from one another; the greater the gap between each of them, the more nature would play an essential role. These discrete structures facilitate a loose, holiday version of family life with lots of outdoor cooking and spontaneous entertaining. The house is also a framework on which Pettena has been able to hang his own artworks and those of others, including a fire surround by Alessandro Mendini (b 1931) and various other design pieces by well-known Italian designer friends.

Jean Nouvel, Serpentine Gallery Pavilion, Kensington Gardens, London, England, 2010.

Though making use of extremely direct language, this industrial collection of walls, planes and jacked-up surfaces succeeded in scrambling activities that suit its park setting. Table tennis, picnics and evening cocktails were all part of the mix. Its attention-grabbing total redness was intended to contrast with the luscious green of Kensington Gardens in summer.

Gianni Pettena, House in Elba 1, Italy, 1978–.

From its Robinson Crusoe beginnings in an inaccessible niche overlooking the sea, this ongoing project parallels the growth according to need of most Italian *poderi* (farmhouses). This is architecture as self-portrait; here Pettena narrates his identity, relations and ideas as an architect. Independent structures house the sleeping quarters while social activities occupy the open spaces between them. Works by many of Pettena's designer friends such as Alessandro Mendini and Ettore Sottsass heighten the sense of discovery.

Summary

These three different types of narrative – binary, sequence and biotopic – result in buildings which resonate on different levels and engage the user or onlooker in a range of imaginative or interactive processes. The binary, that of the dual identity, is the easiest to define, the most purely visual and often the most obviously witty. The sequential encompasses the added factors of time and direction, in a more complex experiential environment. The biotopic,

yet more nuanced but less prescriptive, offers multiple readings and revels
in the coexistence of coherence and diversity. We have seen evidence of the
inspirational qualities that each of these approaches can bring to buildings
and spaces that are narrative-driven in design. I will now present some of my
own built projects and exhibition work, conceived in that spirit.

References

1 Marshall McLuhan, *Understanding Media: The Extensions of Man*, Routledge & Kegan Paul (London), 1964.
2 This notion is explored in depth in Neil Leach (ed), *Rethinking Architecture*, Routledge (London), 1997, and in particular in the chapter by Umberto Eco, 'Function and Sign: the Semiotics of Architecture', pp 173–95.
3 Kevin Lynch, 'The City Image and its Elements', *The Image of the City*, MIT Press (Cambridge, MA), 1960, pp 46–90.
4 See Elisabetta Andreoli and Adrian Forty (eds), *Brazil's Modern Architecture*, Phaidon (London), 2004, pp 91–5.
5 Lynch, op cit, p 99.
6 Ibid, p 91.
7 Francesca Ferguson, 'Architecture Minds the Gap: Berlin's Fragmented Urbanisation', in Markus Miessen and Shumon Basar (eds), *Did Someone Say Participate?*, Revolver (Frankfurt am Main), 2006, pp 126–7.
8 Ibid.
9 Kazuyo Sejima, in *109 Provisional Attempts to Address Six Simple and Hard Questions about What Architects Do Today and Where Their Profession Might Go Tomorrow*, *Hunch* magazine, Issue 6/7 (July 2003), Berlage Institute, Episode Publishers.

5
Practice
in Person

The social and political upheavals of the early 1980s fuelled many of the explorations that led to narrative as an architectural tool. Post-NATO, as my work matured, I looked further afield for references. A good deal of experiment fed into imaginary projects like 'Ecstacity', which served as a motor for the built projects that followed, such as the extension to London's Geffrye Museum (1998) and the National Centre for Popular Music in Sheffield (1999). In partnership with Doug Branson (b 1951), the building phase of the late 1990s culminated in the Body Zone at the Millennium Dome and the first of several contributions to the Venice Architecture Biennale in 2000 as *Ecstacity*, an installation version of my book *Guide to Ecstacity* (published in 2003), in the British Pavilion.[1]

      Similar art-in-architecture projects continued with 'Baby:London' at the 10th Venice Architecture Biennale in 2006, and the following year I exhibited in the 'Global Cities' exhibition at Tate Modern. On a larger scale at the 11th Venice Architecture Biennale in 2008 (curated by architectural critic and educator Aaron Betsky (b 1958)), I built the *Hypnerotosphere* installation in the Corderie dell'Arsenale, the extensive 16th-century buildings that originally housed Venice's naval rope-works and are now one of the main Biennale exhibition spaces. Throughout this period I had alternated between writing, design work, exhibitions and furniture design, often using the work in one of these fields as inspiration for that in another. Even writing, which can be retroactive or a vehicle for the imagination, had an important role for me. In my early teaching days with Bernard Tschumi, we had sequestered literature into our design methodology, and found plenty of stories that seemed to suggest ways of stretching our ability to imagine architectural space.

While being interviewed by a student on the subject of narrative, I gradually realised that her questions were coming from the basis that narrative design starts with writing. I had written a great deal with numerous briefs for students. But my approach as a designer is to include writing in the process of imagining and testing. Projects like the first version of 'Ecstacity' (see chapter 3) were built up from invented words that I mapped into swirling diagrams of dotted lines and arrows. I orchestrated these potent fragments into an idea cloud that could be superimposed on the city, loading the existing urban condition with a magnetic charge of possibility.

Caffè Bongo, Tokyo

The first fully operational, unadulterated piece of narrative architecture I realised was the Caffè Bongo in Tokyo, which opened in 1986 near the busiest pedestrian corner in the world. Having made a successful debut in Tokyo with the Metropole restaurant the year before, the Parco department store in the Shibuya district wanted a café with a bit of European oomph. They knew that the young internationally minded generation was curious about Europe's cocktail of history and fashionable cool.

Branson Coates, Caffè Bongo, Tokyo, Japan, 1986.

Based on a reading of Federico Fellini's *La Dolce Vita*, this overtly layered composition was meant to express Japan's new ability to connect with faraway places. Engaging the film's key opposition between celebrity glamour and the backdrop of Rome's historical bricolage, the interior combined salvaged materials and objects in a twisting choreography of enclosure. On the outside a suspended aircraft wing lightened the blunt interface with the concrete facade above.

In the early 1980s the exchange between Europe and Japan had reached fever pitch. Planeloads of the newly formed London club crowd were being taken to Tokyo to model in ads and fashion shows. Parco's executives also wanted an eye-catching design, one that could compete with the riot of messages on the stores either side of their own.

The search was on for a metaphor for this new internationalism, and one that could provide an architectural vocabulary too. Where better to start, I thought, than with Federico Fellini's iconic film *La Dolce Vita* (1960)? It was the perfect 'narrative' for the design. The film featured the cultural tensions, glamour and internationalism that hit Rome at the beginning of the 1960s. I was captivated by the moment when Anita Ekberg descends from her inbound DC-8 towards a gang of photographers (indeed the first so-called paparazzi) there to meet her. The film unfolds against the bizarre and fabulous backdrop of Roman antiquities that are still lived in today. I asked all my team, including artists and designers I planned to involve in the project, to attend a private screening of the movie at a preview theatre in London.

Caffè Bongo turned out to be NATO made physical. It was an orchestrated collision of references, including the aforementioned aircraft, now reduced to one wing suspended above the window, a two-storey-high wall of fake Roman bricks in which contemporary detritus had been 'buried', and somewhere between, a balcony that was half ancient temple and half

Branson Coates, Katharine Hamnett shop, Sloane Street, London, England, 1987.

With its riot of overlaid references, this store was anything but minimal. The window sported a Tom Dixon triple-decker fish tank, while the inside fused construction-site improvisation – scaffolding and tarpaulins – with elaborate plasterwork and a large Venetian mirror.

aircraft wing. All these elements were composed into a three-dimensional distorted whole that seemed to sway. Bongo visually choreographed people from the street into the space, and then encouraged them to interact with it by picking over the plethora of references and details between cappuccinos.

One could have interpreted this mix as wilful chaos, and in some ways it was. But that's what life was like in Tokyo at the time. It was vital, exciting and contradictory. A little wooden house I often passed had survived the ravages of the 20th century, but found itself wedged between two enormous blocks. To a Japanese way of thinking, this was nothing out of the ordinary. Like the London of the 19th century, Tokyo was itself a narrative experience in which stories of all kinds, eastern and western, were being told at once.

In this project I found a rich source in the archaeology that goes with Rome and the language of flight – of aircraft and airports as the portals of travel, and the crossing of cultural convention. By this time too I was firmly addicted to collaborating with many other creative people, partly because we would egg each other on, and partly because this combination of energies reflected the cities we were living in.

Shops in Knightsbridge, London

In the London of the late 1980s it was the world of fashion that first saw the commercial value in narrative architecture; fashion retail emerged as its perfect testing ground. By the 1990s fashion brands were becoming

Branson Coates, Jigsaw shop, Brompton Road, London, England, 1991.

High ceilings, two levels and a smart location up the road from Harrods charge this flagship with a palatial narrative unfolding around a sweeping central stair. Downstairs has a stable-like simplicity, but the *piano nobile* has a voluptuous cash desk and frescoed frieze that wraps around the room.

truly international and very big business. Leading designers like Paul Smith and Katharine Hamnett wanted to present their clothes in evocative environments, not the practical containers used by high-street stores like Gap and Next. Their intention was to create parallel worlds where you could try on their designs, and safely experiment with your identity. These environments needed to stir up ideas, and lift their function to a level at which anything seemed possible, which is how these designers wanted you to feel in their clothes. The space would limber you up to think laterally, and up your confidence.

In 1987 I designed a shop for Katharine Hamnett in Sloane Street that was the antithesis of her previous flagship, a minimal white and mirrored space by Norman Foster. This time she wanted a cultural cornucopia that combined the street with 18th-century opulence. There were fish tanks in the window designed by Tom Dixon (b 1959). I brought scaffolding and proto-electrical lighting into the mix, and orchestrated all these fragments with the skills I had learnt with NATO and in Tokyo.

Four years later, just around the corner, Jigsaw wanted to upgrade their image. The product was fresh, natural and bathed in Mediterranean light, so I wanted the shops to reflect this by adopting signs of nature – which was the flavour of our first shop for them in Kensington. Subsequently the Knightsbridge shop was modelled on an imaginary Italian palace, with a sweeping staircase, spiral chandelier with suspended glass torsos and, surrounding the entire upper floor, a bucolic frieze painted by British artist Stewart

Nigel Coates, The Wall, Tokyo, Japan, drawing, 1989.

Under the playful supposition that the ancient Romans had reached Tokyo, the remains of a city wall had been redeployed as a multi-tenant building with bars, shops and restaurants on each of its seven storeys. This pastel and pencil drawing splits open the various layers of the building, and invites exploration of it.

Helm (b 1960). The commercial success of these shops proved that 'industrial baroque', as I called it, touched a surprisingly profitable nerve with the public.

The Wall and Art Silo, Tokyo

This creative battery was still fully charged when we were commissioned to design two buildings in Tokyo: The Wall (1989–90) and later the building next door, the Art Silo (1992). Both are replete with visual and spatial contradictions that keep the eye and the mind on the move. They are inexplicable, in that they are inconsistent. The Wall is a response to a contradiction that first came from the client: 'I'd like a building that represents the 20th century but looks as though it's been there for ever.' In reality it was to be a multi-tenant building Tokyo style, with different bars and restaurants on each floor. For the design I came up with a building that had distinct historicist references, and in this sense it is postmodern. But it also had the *bricolage* of earlier Tokyo works, with an aircraft wing on top, a gasometer structure in front, and a huge clock designed by Tom Dixon

Branson Coates, The Wall, Tokyo, Japan, 1990.

The building's main artistic events are situated between its cast-iron and brick facades. These include the interweaving staircase, an 8m-high ceramic sculpture by Grayson Perry and Tom Dixon's large clock, Big Tom.

Nigel Coates, The Wall and Art Silo, Tokyo, Japan, drawing, 1991.

On the street corner adjacent to The Wall is Art Silo, rising like a giant standing figure. A lift runs up the building's spine and individual galleries mimic the softened cone of the human visual field.

that I called Big Tom. The crux of the story was that the Romans had been to Tokyo, and this fragment of Roman wall was all that remained. In pursuit of authenticity, the brick and stone cladding was executed by two local builders I knew from a small village in Tuscany. Its present manifestation reveals all the modifications that this fragment of wall had undergone over the centuries. Its current use as a leisure hub would reinforce a sense of the present, and continue to do so into the 21st century.

Art Silo, however, was to be more body-like in form and character. I thought of it as an erect being that could adopt various kinds of clothing including a coat of many colours and a hat. One of the early sketches for this project lays out this interpretation, with the new building situated halfway between The Wall and a giant figure. The spatial organisation of the building reinforced this apparent simplicity, bringing visitors up to each of its gallery floors via a lift that provided a spine to the whole structure.

'Living Bridges' exhibition

In 1996 Marie Ann Stevens and Peter Murray, curators at the Royal Academy of Arts in London wanted to stage an exhibition about inhabitable bridges like Florence's Ponte Vecchio. The idea had originated in a much more academic form at the Centre Pompidou in Paris. We wanted something lively that would captivate the audience and overcome some of the stilted

Branson Coates, 'Living Bridges' exhibition, Royal Academy of Arts, London, England, 1996.

Identically scaled models told the history and future of the inhabitable bridge along a conceptual river of suitably brown water that meandered through the galleries of the Academy. It was crossed by built structures like the Ponte Vecchio and Kazimir Malevich's unbuilt car park that he designed to span the Seine.

communication of most architectural exhibitions. It was decided that there should be a 'river' – a river that flowed through time rather than space – that would accommodate models of identical scale, starting with Old London Bridge and finishing with a competition to build a new inhabitable bridge in London.

In reality this river was a caravan of waist-high containers with shallow tanks holding suitably brown river-coloured water dramatically spotlit within the gloomy, cavernous spaces of the galleries. These tanks followed a meandering path from room to room like a visitor moving from gallery to gallery while looking at the pictures. But in the darkened galleries, the river was the focus and a timeline along which each of the 24 bridges – whether lost, built or unbuilt – spanned the river.

Every bridge was a model with dozens of brightly painted model people; oversized reproductions of drawings and paintings stood proud of the walls. The river was a rather literal narrative device – not the Thames but any river according to each of the models. I evolved the idea to help match the needs of the exhibition. You had to be able to cross from one side of the river to the other; some models were much larger than others so the river had to swell. I remember there was an argument about the colour of the water: the utility company sponsoring the exhibition wanted blue water, I wanted muddy grey.

Geffrye Museum new wing, London

Visitors to the Geffrye, a museum in East London dedicated to the domestic interior, enter a time tunnel that passes between each of the original almshouses that the displays currently occupy. Our job was to design a new wing (opened 1998) to extend the exhibition space. Maintaining the principle of the room set used throughout the museum, we wanted to build on the existing sequential trajectory and literally give it a twist.

The experience begins in the 1600s in the study of diarist Samuel Pepys (1633–1703), and passes from room to room, century to century, until visitors emerge into a covered 'piazza' that separates the old building from the new. The spatial narrative of the new building elaborates the pace and straight path of the original museum; as it reaches new room settings, this path curves and expands into the full width of the building.

The project plays with context not only spatially but with the vocabulary of the building too. As you emerge into the piazza, you see two gable ends ahead of you, and a gap between them: the entrance to the 20th-century galleries. These are organised on a curve rather than a straight

line, reinforced by the flowing form of the Diagrid glass roof and a wide spiral stair that 'excavates' down towards a lower gallery level. Overall the building combines traditional structures with a sweeping organic choreography that acts as an avatar for the visitor. The 'heavy' brick outer structure celebrates traditional construction with thick timber trusses; a curve in the footprint translates the building into a drum. But for most visitors the new wing is an entirely interior experience, with controlled views into the gardens only at one point in the sequence. Inside I wanted a charm bracelet of vignettes, and outside a surrealist take on Victorian engineering.

Powerhouse::uk, London and National Centre for Popular Music, Sheffield

The Geffrye's combination of progress and rotation extends to two projects with a virtually identical plan, Powerhouse::uk in London (1998) and the National Centre for Popular Music in Sheffield (1999). Powerhouse was a

Nigel Coates, Geffrye Museum, London, England, drawing, 1996.

Visitors cross a glass-roofed bridging space between old and new. Designed to extend the experience of room displays housed in the 18th-century almshouses the museum occupies, the new wing catches this trajectory of the time line and curves an apparently traditional structure into a dynamic loop.

temporary structure at the bottom of the Prime Minister's garden in Horse Guards Parade, and was designed to celebrate the creative industries in Britain. Commissioned by the Department of Trade and Industry, it was one of the first gestures towards design made by the newly elected Labour Government, nominated by some as facilitators of 'Cool Britannia'. This large inflatable structure was designed and fully commissioned in little over six months including the exhibits inside the four silver drums organised around a cross-shaped central space.

Visitors would first enter this central space, and then be faced with four equal choices, four galleries each with their own distinct theme. Four aspects of British creativity were explored: Lifestyle, Communicating, Learning and Networking. Overall these spaces were attempting to show how designers work in a more interactive and interdisciplinary way than ever before. Architecturally the idea was to get at the sequential experience by short-circuiting it, disorienting the visitor and raising the experiential threshold. In addition its semi-industrial quality gave the building a sense of autonomy that challenged the visitor to a heightened spatial awareness.

Branson Coates, Powerhouse::uk, Whitehall, London, England, 1998.

Conceived, designed and built in six months, this inflatable, steel and fabric structure housed the best of creative Britain in four drum-shaped galleries. They defined a very graphic plan that sat on the royal route through Whitehall. From the central crossing visitors were presented with an equal choice between the galleries.

Branson Coates, National Centre for Popular Music, Sheffield, England, 1999.

The mother ship of Powerhouse: four drums heaved up from the ground define an urban marker. Visitors have a choice of entry points but reach the upper level from the centre of the crossing. A glass and steel roof projects outwards at four cardinal points as a sign of the complex rotational space inside.

Branson Coates, Powerhouse::uk, Whitehall, London, England, 1998: interior.

Each drum activated the subject matter with its installation; in 'Lifestyle' objects were displayed on a luggage conveyer, while the 'Communicating' section was based on an urban landscape loosely inspired by London made from books and packaging.

While Powerhouse teemed with ideas and talent inside it, the National Centre for Popular Music suffered from the outset from uncertainty about the contents. Our design was an ambitious machine based on the four-drum plan, a direct response to the original brief to provide four galleries housing exhibits reflecting the culture of pop. The museum's producers wanted to key-in to the vibrant local music scene in Sheffield, and give pop more of a sense of history. They needed a landmark to house these ambitions, one that fitted the new image of Sheffield. They would have achieved all three had the displays been up to the standard of the building.

Our idea was to jack four circular galleries up to first-floor level, and bring visitors up a wide staircase in the centre of the building. They were to be covered in stainless steel (a material of huge importance locally as Sheffield was a global leader in steel production from the 19th until the late 20th century) and be topped with streamlined extract ducts that would pull stale air out into the atmosphere. These constantly turn mechanically in order to align downwind. Like Powerhouse, visitors would write their own script, choosing which gallery to enter first. Unfortunately there were not enough them, which is why after only six months the museum closed. It later became a popular music venue as The Hub. Nevertheless the building successfully combines geometry and imagery to link it to extreme opposites of Sheffield culture. It is an urban marker, an extension of the gridded street pattern surrounding it and a very earnest attempt at using its sustainable credentials as part of its sign.

Nigel Coates, *Mixtacity*, 'Global Cities' exhibition, Tate Modern, London, England, 2007: overview.

This attempt at visualising a multicultural regeneration of the Thames Gateway took the form of a collection of narrative architectural set pieces arranged inside an 8m-long vitrine that spanned a corner of the exhibition. Its language combined digitally generated architecture with found objects, biscuits and packs of razor blades in a playful representation of the future city.

Mixtacity

Nigel Coates, *Mixtacity*, 'Global Cities' exhibition, Tate Modern, London, England, 2007: Dagenhamburg.

East London's urban centre focuses either side of a new bridge over the Thames at the place previously named Dagenham. Cupped hands express an enterprising yet shared human spirit. Each of the fingers houses offices, shops and restaurants; this area has the vitality and intensity of Shibuya in Tokyo.

Following the success of the 2006 Venice Architecture Biennale directed by Ricky Burdett and dedicated to the theme of 'Cities, Architecture and Society', a distilled version of it was staged in the Turbine Hall at Tate Modern in 2007. Myself and two other architects – Zaha Hadid (b 1950) and Rem Koolhaas – were invited to devise installations that would contribute urban vision, and freely explore what cities might become. My given theme was diversity, which I chose to interpret in a version of the Thames Gateway, the vast area of potential development land stretching east from London on both sides of the river that was the subject of much speculation and impending disappointment at the time. Instead of looking at the entire area under consideration by the quango set up to promote it, I chose to look at a strip of the north bank of the Thames, from Canary Wharf to Rainham Marshes, from the point of view of the exaggerated multiculturalism likely to accompany the predicted million new inhabitants.

Nigel Coates, *Mixtacity*, 'Global Cities' exhibition, Tate Modern, London, England, 2007: Smoking Gun Heights, render of the digital model behind the 3D print used for the installation.

This compound for eco-evangelists sits at a strategic curve in the river. The waving digital outer surfaces of this complex contrast with the lift and service structures at the centre of each tower; each one is based on an oversized firearm pointing upwards towards the sky.

Like all future visions, *Mixtacity* tried to stimulate the imagination by supposing that it already existed – but in miniature. We built a large model spreading through an L-shaped vitrine that encouraged visitors to peer into its make-believe world of bright colours and bizarre buildings. Although made up from an eclectic collection of new designs and *objets trouvés*, it was unmistakable as a city landscape.

This urban cabinet of curiosities incorporated a spread of digitally designed story-architectures realised as rapid prototypes. The manifesto-like structures were set amongst other buildings made of sweets, biscuits, razor blades and electrical components alongside plastic figures, chess pieces, model buses and helicopters, all laid against a photographic bird's-eye view of this section through East London and the Thames.

Mixtacity emphasised identity, difference and place. The aim was to make a city full of the unknown and the unexpected, such as the buildings made from scaled-up body parts. In this imaginary world, Central Londoners would certainly have heard of Smoking Gun Heights or Barking Towngate, and the massive finger towers at the centre of Dagenhamburg, the new symbol of the Gateway.

These hybrids and crossovers may not be a replacement for the historic depth of most cities across Britain, yet they are capable of expressing the kind of complexity so often omitted from most new development. Without ever claiming this work to be art, it certainly was a critical work with a high component of imagination. It built on people's familiarity with architecture, if not with designing it, and harnessed the public's playful fascination with miniatures – the sense that artistry could, and should, have a role in architecture.

Hypnerotosphere

When curator Aaron Betsky came up with the challenging theme for the 2008 Venice Architecture Biennale, 'Out There: Architecture Beyond Building', the post-millennial building boom was already crashing down around developers' ears. In Betsky's view it was time to question the validity of building, and go deeper into the value of architectural experiment. I was to be part of the Corderie dell'Arsenale show 'At Home in the Modern World', an attempt to overcome the alienating effect of most built architecture. I wanted to build a temple to the fully sensing – and sensuous – body.

For some time I had been fascinated by the exceptional Renaissance literary work, the *Hypnerotomachia Poliphili*, which was published anonymously in a lavishly illustrated volume printed in Venice at the end of the 15th century.[2] Perhaps it could be the starting point to fulfil the brief for participating in the Biennale. I wanted to offset this historical and visionary work with the lack of vision in watered-down Modernism, and chose a humungous and equally notorious public housing project in Rome called Corviale (1972–82)

Francesco Colonna, 'The Rites of Faunus', *Hypnerotomachia Poliphili*, Venice, Italy, 1499, p 195.

The lavishly illustrated text includes seductive if hermetic architectural situations that occur to the protagonist while searching for his love in the mysterious and threatening 'dark forest'. This bower housing a herm of Faunus is the focus of orgiastic sacrifice.

Nigel Coates, *Hypnerotosphere*, sketch, 2008.

As an example of architecture beyond building, this installation explored being 'at home' in your own body; its circular 'sphere' cocooned the public in a subtly erotic space shared with a landscape of body inspired furniture and a 360° movie about the human ability to perform cycles of construction and destruction.

to alternate with the *Hypnerotomachia* to form the background – the 'dark wood' in the original text – from which to explore the body as architecture.

The initial sketch was leading me towards a visceral abstraction, and it eschews architectural definition. It is more of an interior conscribed, and inspired in part by Francis Bacon's (1909–92) harrowing portraits in which the 'figure' sits within a conceptual cube of lines drawn in space. Here the existing building would provide the equivalent of Bacon's recurring cube; my

Federico Gorio, Piero Maria Lugli, Giulio Sterbini, and Michele Valori, coordinated by Mario Fiorentino, Corviale public housing, Rome, Italy, 1972–82.

This relentless public housing project exemplifies ideological mistakes by architects. Housing 14,000 people over its 400m length, it bears little resemblance to the complexity of the urbs that it tries to supersede. The film includes clips of it representing the dark forest of contemporary architecture.

installation would sit between the last four columns along the colonnade that defines the central spine of the Corderie exhibition space. I intended my installation, the *Hypnerotosphere*, to feel like a Tardis, a circular space that could transcend its enclosure as a consequence of the unexpected scale and content inside it. The real subject was being 'at home' in your own body, and the fusion of the senses in terms of the viewer and the objects viewed.

Whereas in the *Hypnerotomachia*, the story leads Poliphilo and the reader through a variety of situations, in this Biennale project the viewer entered a semi-enclosed space with a total-surround screen suspended at chest height above the floor, onto which was projected a film of two male dancers, a collaboration with film director John Maybury (b 1958). The dancers expressed architectural processes through movement in four short pieces: 'Liquid Landscapes', 'Skin Wraps Flesh', 'Constructions' and 'Tumbling Towers'. Multiples of the film were projected on a circular screen enveloping the viewer in a landscape of leather furniture inspired by the human body.

The furniture represents two physical bodies interacting, like the two dancers in the film. I studied the two key parts of an English saddle – the

Nigel Coates, *Hypnerotosphere*, 'At Home in the Modern World', Corderie dell'Arsenale, 11th Venice Architecture Biennale, Venice, Italy, 2008.

Movie and furniture in a circular setting combined well with six chandeliers that, hanging in the centre of the space, partially obscured the projection. The installation paralleled the composition of the principle rooms of a classic Venetian palazzo. Chandeliers, frescoes and furniture combined forces to ricochet their images, meanings, light and texture between one another.

Nigel Coates, saddle from
Hypnerotosphere.

As a generative form, the
saddle emphasises the
contact between two living
bodies: the rider and the
horse. This piece accentuates
the outer wrapping surface
and the inner cushions that
normally sit either side of
the horse's spine. Here they
are enlarged to become a
body in their own right with
connotations of both male
and female genitalia.

wrapping outer surface and beneath
it the 'cushions' that make contact
with the horse – and adapted these
to make several upholstered objects
that carry this duality of contact
within their forms. Each of the four
pieces applies these two elements
in different ways. The saddle, sofa,
chaise and table are variations on
each other.

A group of crystal lamps
floated above the furniture in such a way as to partially obscure the film;
each light supported a miniature city made up of shapes similar to those of
the furniture. The effect was to bind furniture, the lamps/cityscapes and the
film into one fluid condition. The atmosphere was temple-like. The shiny
black floor made watery reflections of the visitors, the furniture pieces, the
light sculptures and projections; by accident I had created the paradigm of
a frescoed Venetian interior complete with Murano chandeliers.

Nigel Coates and
John Maybury,
Hypnerotosphere, 2008:
film still.

The movie has four phases of
body movement performed
by two male dancers: 'Liquid
Landscapes', 'Skin Wraps
Flesh', 'Construction' and
'Tumbling Towers'. These
perform basic moves equally
visible in the furniture and in
architecture generally.

The narrative thread

My ever-increasing engagement with narrative in architecture, then,
has involved turning for inspiration to sources from archaeology to
anthropomorphism, and from film to flight. By providing associative triggers
to enhance the visitor's experience, I have tried to create hybrid environments
where identity can be experimented with and ideas stirred up. In some
projects I have explored the use of sequence narrative to visually choreograph
visitors into and around spaces; in others I have the choice of path wide open.

I found that there is no harm
in including elements that
at first appear incongruous
or contradictory – on the
contrary, they can add to the
user's experience of the space,
by keeping the mind constantly
active and questioning.
Narrative offers endlessly rich
and beguiling possibilities, and
has become a driving force in
all my work, in architecture,

interiors, product design and elsewhere. What is more, its influence appears to be becoming ever more pervasive in the perception of the wider urban environment, and indeed in the increasingly powerful virtual realm – as the next chapter will examine.

Nigel Coates, chandeliers from *Hypnerotosphere*.

Six chandeliers hang in the centre of the space to create the impression of clouds that carry Lilliputian cities. Buildings are formed by the same shapes as in the furniture, with steel angles, double cushions and computer-designed wrapping forms realised as rapid prototypes.

References

1 Nigel Coates, *Guide to Ecstacity*, Laurence King (London), 2003.
2 Francesco Colonna, *Hypnerotomachia Poliphili*, Venice, 1499, first English edition published in London, 1592.

6

Pure 'Narrativity'

From Europe, New York always seemed to mark an urban apotheosis. With the long perspective of exile in London, British-born American poet Ezra Pound (1885–1972) wrote of its particular intensity: 'No urban night is like the night there ... Squares after squares of flame, set up and cut into the aether.'[1] For Irish writer James Joyce (1882–1941) the city – in the form of Dublin – provides the tumultuous, immersive world that is the setting for *Ulysses* (1922).[2] And for Futurists like Giacomo Balla (1871–1958) and Umberto Boccioni (1882–1916) the pounding intensity of the urban machine is itself a paradigm of nature, and key to its excitement and liberating energy. This embracing of ecstatic pandemonium has continued through to present times. Rem Koolhaas, for example, celebrates 'congestion' as an urban quality.[3] The city's complexity, confusion and apparent autonomy might be the key to its attraction. 'Architecture' is more likely to be found in the totality of the city than in the singular efforts of the architect.

This staccato effect of urban experience comes through in, and often inspired, early avant-garde cinema in which filmmakers, lacking the technology to dissolve one scene into another, could fade the image to black or abruptly jump cut from one to another. Sergei Eisenstein's (1898–1948) montage device was indeed a way of creating the illusion of continuous movement and spatial contiguity by simply splicing different scene stock together. The Russian filmmaker would try to diminish architecture as object, and increase its experience. But the cameraman's view – as well as the director's – was of special significance for one architectural theorist who cited filmic assemblage as a paradigm of the spatial construct.

As a way of contextualising architectural thinking, in *Collage City*, Colin Rowe observes: 'Magician and surgeon compare to painter and cameraman. The painter maintains in his work a natural distance from reality, the cameraman penetrates deeply into its web. There is a tremendous difference between pictures they maintain. That of the painter is a total one, that of the cameraman consists of multiple fragments which are assembled under a new law.'[4]

Meanwhile Italian film director Pier Paolo Pasolini (1922–75) was less concerned with spatial and temporal illusion. Indeed, often continuous scenes jump from location to location with little attempt to hide the fact. His focus is frequently on bringing the audience and the actors closer to one another, objectifying the frame – as in close-up, zoom – to emphasise the neurotic condition of the actor, who in turn brings out the unstable side of the audience. It is tempting to liken the frame to the formal aspects of architecture in its repetition, geometry and resolute materiality.

Piranesi's *Vedute*

Proto-cineaste Giovanni Battista Piranesi (1720–78) would freely blend the spoils of archaeological material with a high degree of creative invention.

Giovanni Battista Piranesi, second frontispiece etching, *Vedute di Roma*, 1748.

With this image Piranesi succeeds in accentuating the phenomenal; in an elaborate capriccio of archaeological artefacts that would have been familiar at the time, this frontispiece exaggerates the dramatic effect by incorporating tiny figures and vigorous vegetation.

Many of his prints illustrate Rome in its decadent heyday, but with a certain theatrical push. His *Vedute di Roma* ('Views of Rome', 1748), commissioned by the Roman bookseller Fausto Amidei, incorporate such exaggerations of scale that a disciple would have been disappointed when seeing these locations in the flesh. Although within the tradition of the measured drawing, thoroughly recording every detail, his compositions embrace the state of decay that Rome had reached by the mid-18th century. To solicit all our senses, these prints enlist nature at its most flamboyant. He understood the taste of the Grand Tour and, to satisfy its participants, had to play up the scale, the decay and rampant undergrowth.

The frontispiece of the *Vedute* takes this 'improvement' to extremes, with a capriccio of architectural and sculptural fragments that did exist but, instead of being found together, were drawn from various locations across the city. At the centre sits the allegorical figure of Rome, and the names of illustrious people who had contributed to Rome's power and civilisation are engraved on some of the blocks of stone. As an image that foregrounds the plates that follow, it affirms the power of the imagination necessary to fully benefit from the engravings, and ultimately the city itself – which, compared to any other at the time, was one that incorporated a perspective on time in a unique, narrative way. As French poet Voltaire (1694–1778) said: '*Le superflu, chose très nécessaire*' ('The superfluous, a very necessary thing').[5]

Delirious New York

In the early years of his career Rem Koolhaas worked closely with his wife Madelon Vriesendorp (b 1945) to explore New York in terms of human attraction and emotion, interpreting skyscrapers as individual figures – and lovers. They meet, fall in love and sleep together. In an image of the mythical origins of Manhattan, Liberty lies devastated, de-torched and de-crowned, and gives way to the newly confident skyscrapers that stand erect alongside her supine body.

This cycle of vivid illustrations came to accompany Koolhaas's book *Delirious New York*.[6] On its pages, he unravels the Freudian weakness, ambition and imaginative qualities of cities in dialogue with Vriesendorp's ability to draw them. Closer to the fanciful interpretative work of Piranesi than the driving progress of Modernist architects, together they brought a new kind of imagination into the field of architectural discourse. Indeed, *Delirious New York* set up the means to incorporate the imagination and intellect in much of Koolhaas's later work with OMA. Even the title 'Delirious New York' suggests that the city possesses its own psychological profile, and that it has the capacity not only to be rational (the grid, the skyscraper) but to be delirious (the ambition, the rivalry, the seduction), which for a city were unexpected Freudian qualities.

The technique of reconfiguring and reorganising elements certainly introduces a fictitious dimension into the territory of 'truth' normally expected of the architect. Yet too much truth may not only be unexciting, but will surely fail to stretch the imagination beyond cliché and the tried and tested. The classic manoeuvring of the given towards a more seductive form is on the one hand thought to be false, but culture would move very little without it. There is a very valid argument for an artistic interpretation of architecture to stretch the medium out of its comfort zone, and be all the more persuasive if it is not built.

There is indeed a valid reality to the unbuilt, a theme that was explored in depth at the 11th Venice Architecture Biennale in 2008. Curator Aaron Betsky consigned built architecture to virtually an interference in the

Madelon Vriesendorp, *The Ecstasy of Mrs Calgari*, 1974.

As part of an extended series featuring the two most iconic skyscrapers in New York, Liberty is stretched out on the bed of Manhattan, toppled from her upright pose with her torch cast accidentally aside. Her giant presence renders the buildings of the city toys in an urban game of triumph and compliance.

culture of architecture. 'Most buildings are ugly, useless and wasteful. Yet architecture is beautiful – it can place us in the world in a way no other art can.'[7] Like literature, like movies, a fictional architecture can stimulate our thoughts about the world we already occupy by reconfiguring what we already know. Betsky continues: '(Architectural) experimentation can take the form of momentary constructions, visions of other worlds, or the building blocks of a better world. This real fiction can turn up some very real questions, and postulate what other possibilities there might be above and beyond solutions to more prosaic social problems.'[8]

Urban fiction

As film director John Maybury (b 1958) commented at an event discussing architecture and movies, 'architecture and cinema share the same cocktail of magic realism and deceptive illusion in that both are essentially fraudulent'.[9] In the lottery of 20th-century expression, the medium of cinema was bound to disturb and supersede Modernist thinking, and overlay reality with a fictional heightening of the urban project. Conversely, instead of architecture merely appearing as a background within film, suspension of disbelief would have a bearing on how architecture was itself created.

Strangely it is only in the postmodern era, from the early 1980s to the present, that the full effects of cinematic communication can be felt in architecture. This transformation continues with the intersection of all forms of computer-based media. In a world of YouTube and Facebook, the moving image becomes increasingly cross platform and independent from the movie theatre, embracing everyone as a potential moviemaker and storyteller. We move uncannily into Ballardian territory.

The fictional constructs of JG Ballard (1930–2009) make the most of portraying a complete world that, at first, seems to mirror reality. As Merlin Coverley argues: 'Ballard does not so much invent new buildings as use banal and authorless possible buildings to construct elaborate allegories of contemporary life in which the protagonists are not only subject to boredom, but to extreme forms of behaviour that increasingly reflect the violent and sexualised imagery that surrounds us.'[10]

Seismic shifts in social language are bound to affect architecture in multi-various ways, not least through changing attitudes to sex and sexual orientation. Any hint of erotic content is still taboo in the world of architecture, yet sexual experience can be a powerful driver for artistic expression, including architecture. As Aaron Betsky has written: 'Out of the recesses of the self [queer space] constructs a mirror in which you appear, then dissolves into orgasm. What I am calling queer space is that which appropriates certain aspects of the material world in which we live, composes them into an unreal or artificial space, and uses this counterconstruction to create the free space of orgasm that dissolves the material world.'[11] His view, and a very useful one in architecture, is that in its very nature, queer space is something that is not built, only implied, and usually invisible. In fact any form of sexual desire qualifies the world around you, and shapes how the relatively neutral frameworks of buildings are subject to other more experiential spatial relations. Sex is itself a narrative driver, and an effective paradigm for many others.

Of course sex is not always the motive for social encounter. Friendship, community and salesmanship all make use of the dynamic field of architecture in the drive towards their goals. According to cultural critic Camille Paglia (b 1947), the Lady Gaga phenomenon signals an end to eroticism. 'Gaga's fans are marooned in a global technocracy of fancy gadgets but emotional poverty. Everything is refracted for them through the media. They have been raised in a relativistic cultural vacuum where chronology and sequence as well as distinctions of value have been lost or jettisoned.'[12] But one wonders whether Paglia has misunderstood the mood of 21st-century youth, who having been bombarded with the materialistic and over-sexualised values of their parents are actually happy to adopt a ludic mantle of unedited signs of innocence. Veering away from commodified sex, younger people may feel more comfortable in the protected territory of digital social networking.

Conversely we can pursue behavioural norms in virtual space, as is the case with computer gaming. The game environment posits a plausible yet invented context that is satisfyingly 'real'. Indeed, we live ever more frequently in digitally generated contexts; many of the events we experience take place in other times and in virtual places. Google Earth takes these phenomena to the extreme, where real places that have never been visited can be explored through a variety of intersecting criteria for which the 'map' is little more than a framework for other data, including information about restaurants, shopping and public services.

In the hypothetical worlds of TV and computer games, reality and fiction intertwine and proliferate in a shower of communication – a phenomenon famously explored by French philosopher Jean Baudrillard (1927–2007).[13] Many introduce war conditions into an otherwise familiar city environment, where there is no evidence of ordinary people doing ordinary urban things. For the sake of the game, the city can be emptied to facilitate a simulated war. Players move around these virtual spaces with ease, immersed in narratives of warfare in Iraq or Afghanistan. Yet the spatial language, the way you glide down streets and around buildings, is a sublimation of the familiar one you use on the streets of your own town.

Evidently the fiction in the following artistically contained architectural projects needs to enlist a level of realism into its mix. In works of the imagination the three-sided matrix context/use/narrative (see p 84) still applies, but the context part will be as invented as the other two. Each component needs to have just as good a fit with the other two as it would for a buildable design. The essential configuration of these ingredients, and the skill with which they are handled, replaces any need for style – minimal, maximal or otherwise. In a discussion about the validity of purely hypothetical work, it follows that familiar components need to be exaggerated, offsetting any risk of implausibility that purely artistic work may incur.

The imaginary project also has the need to induce artistic experience, and for a magical ingredient that lifts it free from the dangers of indulgence. As Carlo Mollino says: 'I'm ashamed to say, the inability to explain the scenarios of art, resides in the nature of art itself. In fact only when a work is inexplicable can we indeed be sure that we are in the presence of a work of art. This ineffable quality is the mark of its authenticity.'[14] And according to author DBC Pierre:

> People still want naturalism, but naturalism is about credibility and credibility
> is not where we live right now. The tools that writers use to give their novels
> credibility and gravity are no longer employed in our culture. Things do not
> need to be connected the way they once were in the novel. Nowadays, we
> need things that shimmer on the surface and have tendrils that reach below so
> you can see to a certain depth.[15]

Architecture as street theatre

In the early 1970s, when interest in conceptual art was at its height, it was also a bad time for architects in practice. Any architect who was aware of counterculture moved towards the methods more frequently used by artists. Ugo La Pietra (b 1938) and Gianni Pettena were two young Italian architects caught up in the rethink that become Radical Architecture. Pettena had spent time in America, where he formulated his ideas about the autonomy of architecture as a state of mind. His projects there such as the Ice Houses and the Clay House (see chapter 2) transformed ordinary structures into large temporary sculptures. In his words: 'I don't sell my love to build a public park. My idea of architecture is pure because it does not deal with existing in the real world. I prefer my architecture to tell stories. It is meant to be food for the brain, and not an instrument for practical function.'[16]

Ugo La Pietra also promoted architecture through conceptual works such as the 'Abitare la Città' projects (1962–82) and the pages of the magazines he edited like *In* and *Progettare Inpiù*.[17] Published or performed, his work re-examined the multiple ways people behave in cities, and how individual desires break away from the guide rails that architects try to impose. In one work, *Il Commutatore* ('The Transformer', 1970), La Pietra uses his own body inclined on a hinged stand to 'occupy' a road. As well as questioning the architectural system, he addressed the urban scale of design by subjecting ordinary objects to artistic adaptation. Exploring the gap between the self, the domestic environment and the city, his work narrates an existential biotopic field that overlaps ideology and actuality. The conventional object of architecture is reduced to little more than an encumbrance.

Minutes after the picture of La Pietra was taken for *Il Commutatore*, the clapboard prop would have been gone without trace. A more lingering and shared memory was left behind by *The Sultan's Elephant*, an extravagant performance created by leading French street art company Royal de Luxe

Ugo La Pietra, *Il Commutatore*, 1970.

Transgressing boundaries is a recurring theme in La Pietra's body of work, often contrasting the routes and confines that ordinary people choose over those that are imposed on them. In this ephemeral architectural act, he used his own body as a wall that cuts across the path of oncoming cars.

Royal de Luxe, *The Sultan's Elephant*, London, England, 2006.

Spread over an entire weekend, the event developed an elaborate narrative beginning with the arrival of a giant marionette in a rocket that had mysteriously landed. Over the days that followed, the giant elephant paraded through the streets of central London, as if performing a ritual of urban renewal.

(founded in 1979 by Jean-Luc Courcault). Commissioned by the cities of Nantes and Amiens to mark the 2005 centenary of the death of author Jules Verne (1828–1905) – best known for fantastical novels *Twenty Thousand Leagues under the Sea* (1870) and *Around the World in Eighty Days* (1873) – it was brought to the streets of central London in May 2006. Beginning on a Thursday evening with the 'crash' of a rocket into Waterloo Place, this performance spanned the following three days.

The key narrative involved a Sultan, the girl of his dreams and a time-travelling elephant, which was so large that traffic lights and bollards had to be removed from the streets to allow its passage. Seeing this giant elephant dwarf familiar buildings, jolts the image of the city, and reconfigures assumptions of the environment and our place in it. Some forty 'puppeteers' operated the elephant alone.

On a scale and ambition of triumphal parades, royal weddings and annual festivals like the Carnival in Rio de Janeiro, *The Sultan's Elephant's* power lies in its otherness. Not architecture by any definition of the term, it nevertheless had an architectural dimension of a very urban kind: sweeping slowly through the streets in a protracted act of renewal, the performance had not only forced normal urban functions to be suspended, but caused memories of the ordinary and the predictable to be briefly obfuscated by the extraordinary. In its Lilliputian inversion of scales, it re-energised the city by challenging its scale, its permanence and its hierarchies. Occasionally disturbed and distanced, the city can be all the better for it.

The communications-loaded city

From the creators of computer games to postmodern image-makers, the limits of the urban environment fascinate many artists. In a third example of artists' reflections upon the city, at first Akira Yamaguchi's (b 1969) highly crafted drawings seem to conform to the traditional techniques of 19th-century Japanese artists who documented the urban landscape.[18] Looking more closely, all kinds of details emerge – evidence of 21st-century life appears everywhere, gnawing at and feeding off the larger structures. In their tangle of city life, other, more historical urban landscapes incorporate Hell's Angels riding through on monstrous bikes; and in more modern landscapes, you might find the opposite – a coolie with heavy baskets slung from buckled shoulders. Among the cranes in a reworking of Roppongi, a tower under construction sprouts a traditional pagoda from its peak.

To revise the zoning and functionalist principles expounded by Le Corbusier in his 1943 *Athens Charter*, Andrea Branzi put forward a new version based on the coexistence of all social and productive ingredients in an 'infinite' layered condition that combines all the necessary physical and communication environments that a society needs – 'an "infinite" that must exist in our mind, in our psyche, before existing in reality: mind and psyche are the only possible territories for the refounding of architecture.'[19]

Exhibited at the 2010 Venice Architecture Biennale, Branzi's *New Athens Charter* (2009) recommends a 'weak urbanization', envisaging 'hybrid, semi-urban and semi-agricultural places'.[20] The *No-Stop City* (see chapter 2) which he conceived as a member of Archizoom had begun in the

late 1960s as a Marxist Utopia but, over an extended period of continual revision, developed into a paradigm of the communications-loaded city in which we now live. We read in the Seventh recommendation: 'Interpret the

Akira Yamaguchi, Tokei (Tokyo): Hiroo and Roppongi, drawing, 2002.

This exquisite apparently traditional Edo image is laced with surprise details in its intricate web: the modern tower at the centre of this seething late-night district sports cranes and a traditional temple structure on the roof. Beneath the clouds post-war buildings line the streets, and contemporary Japanese life appears to have changed very little as a result of the building boom.

Andrea Branzi, *New Athens Charter*, 12th Venice Architecture Biennale, Venice, Italy, 2010.

Whatever artefacts become part of these urban scenarios, being reflected in mirrors in every direction renders them architectural. They both represent and reflect themselves; they are object and sign simultaneously.

city as a place where architecture is not a visual presence, but a "sensorial, experiential, immaterial" reality; a place of computer relations and virtual economies; an anthropological area in constant renewal, movement, replacement.'[21] This reverberates with Marshall McLuhan's observation from 50 years earlier: 'The media are "extensions" of human senses, bodies and minds'; this is a place where narratives are constantly forming and reforming according to the ebb and flow of daily life.[22] And in the Ninth recommendation: 'Consider the city as a "genetic laboratory"; interpret the city as a "factory of life"; place of genome exchanges, sexual experiences, development of one's own gene; cities of humans, bodies, flows of sperm, births and deaths.'[23]

Branzi has repeatedly used mirrors to edge his models; we look down into their endless condition, a repetition no matter how formal or informal the model may be. While versions of this ongoing project from the late 1960s were orthogonal, later manifestations have a much more relaxed integration of nature into their matrix. Rules, it would seem, can be used to establish freedom as well as to constrain it. These theoretical environments emphasise the illusory nature of the heterogeneous city. In reality, Branzi suggests, there is no escape from the system of society. To embrace it ensures citizens the benefits of its freedom.

Sub-urban overload

This contradictory aspect of urban systems, like the faults and aberrations incorporated into the world described in Ridley Scott's film *Blade Runner* (1982), moved a step closer towards disturbance in Nicola Koller's *This Sceptred Isle* (2003–6), a graduation project at London's Royal College of Art that eventually became a short movie. Apparently one of the most widespread disorders suffered by the inhabitants of suburbia is depression. How could suburbia be reconfigured? One way is to re-plan the outer city to make use of the soporific effects of driving.

Koller proposed a 'carpet' of swirling motorways 'for the pleasure of driving' supported on pilotis that rise brutally from the housing estates on the outskirts of London. Here every house has an SUV parked out front. To overcome their depression, inhabitants of this 'advanced' suburbia can self-medicate by driving endlessly and senselessly, apart from participating

Nicola Koller and Squint Opera, film still from *Driving with the Joneses: This Sceptred Isle*, 2006.

In this dystopian view of 2020 Britain, SUVs are parked outside identical homes with motorways hovering above. Residents avert their boredom by driving in the hope of spotting one of the bovine targets that drivers can shoot down digitally from their vehicles.

Nicola Koller, plan for *This Sceptred Isle*, 2003.

In this drawing created by Koller as part of her *This Sceptred Isle* project, a dense flying carpet of motorway junctions is 'borrowed' by the designer from various locations across Britain. These provide a leisure facility for depressed suburban inhabitants who live in identical homes beneath the pilotis.

in a game conducted while driving. On-board navigation systems would be combined with a warlike targeting of 'cows' that appear virtually and suddenly to the drivers cruising along the elevated motorways above their homes. A 'hit' equates to a reward such as a ration of prime-quality beef that can be taken home and shared with the family. Like homeopathy, her treatment goes to the heart of the problem and exaggerates it with a dark and slightly feverish portrayal. Using the medium of film, Koller generated a realistic portrayal of archetypal residents, whose life at home is given meaning by the neighbourly rivalry expressed by their obsession with SUVs. This 10-minute movie introduces us to a typical family and how they make sense of their lives by 'hunting' cows along the roadside.

This is clearly not the kind of architecture that has a measurable contribution to make to society, but a critique that has a value by looking in from the outside. Rather than allying itself with architects, it takes architecture as its medium of expression that is open to contamination by popular media. Its audience is not so much architects but the public in general. Koller highlights the major shifts in cultural aspiration, and as a dystopic consequence, suggests the need to put hyperconsumer culture on the back burner.

Urban visionaries

There is a weapon in the iPhone game Angry Birds that boomerangs back towards its target. When you fire it you have to anticipate this returning, and narrative work can have such mechanisms built into it too. The work of multidisciplinary Dutch collective Atelier Van Lieshout (or AVL) sets out to build boomerang effects into artistic language. The more 'crazy' the ideas, the more they seem to elucidate the reality of everyday life. Members of AVL are not afraid to go wholeheartedly against any norms of taste or convention. Their

Atelier Van Lieshout, *SlaveCity* Boardroom, 2007.

This ongoing dystopian project mirrors the sinister workings of society, and is graphically illustrated on a black dinner service set for a congressional dinner. The nearest plate illustrates an operating theatre, one of the masochistic scenarios that describe the life of the inhabitants of the visionary *SlaveCity* as well as their environments.

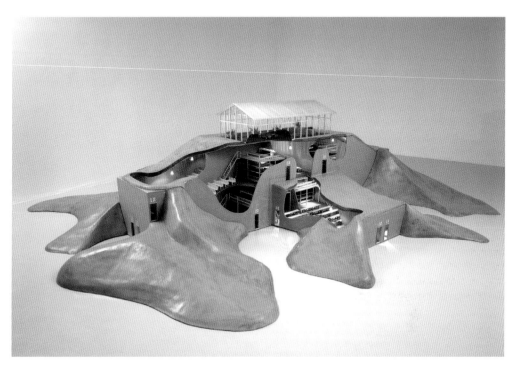

Atelier Van Lieshout, *SlaveCity*, Female Slave University, 2006.

In parallel with *SlaveCity*'s similar Male Slave facility, this large model depicts the education centre of this elaborate sustainable critique of contemporary society. An inhabited hill combines 12 auditoria and sleeping quarters. The greenhouse on top is a meeting room for the professors.

oversized structures have the feel of bandages wrapped around swollen limbs. They make liberal use of aggressive colours, they posit ironic combinations of incompatible activities, like sports and drinking. Despite these programmatic clashes, they often mimic mainstream architectural production. They make buildings out of bodies, and bodies out of buildings. There is a sense that the permanent can always be moved and the movable be permanent. They tangle references such that the context/use/narrative triad allows the migration of signs from each of these three fields to the other two.

In *SlaveCity*, an all-embracing ongoing project they begun in 2005, Joep van Lieshout (b 1963) and his atelier work within the principle that the environment can be shaped through our desire rather than submitting to the false social responsibility of the architect. They are slowly realising a dystopian vision of a city in which all the inhabitants accept their role in the hive. They suggest that Modernism is indeed a kind of enslavement and, despite its thresholds of hope and aspiration, always has its undoing built in. AVL's work stands apart from the mainstream in order to hit harder at the core.

Adopting a gritty feel for reality that is alien to most architecture, there is no accepting convention in any aspect of AVL's work. Many of their projects are full-size constructions. Some oversized bodies also turn out to be places to live in, as though the caravan has mutated into a body part or vice versa. Or else there are drawings that are objects, maps that are furniture or lights or tables. In their hands the apparent sophistication of our society tumbles into a tribal state of survival and uncertainty.

While studying the effects of globalisation for his 2006 Royal College of Art graduation project, Tomas Klassnik saw an inventive way of providing more building space in an otherwise overcrowded City of London. Why not use the empty space above the many churches to build offices? Hanging from a crane hook, the *Desktopolis* tower hovers above Saint Botolph's, Aldgate. Inside, Klassnik proposes a new kind of workplace where disagreements and rivalries can be resolved in 'a new pattern of social organisation assembled beneath a sky of acoustic ceiling tiles'.[24]

Exhibited at 'Baby:London', the RCA's contribution to the 10th Venice Architecture Biennale (2006), *Desktopolis* aggregates an elaborate biotopic narrative with three overlaid – or interlocking – systems of tropes: the first is the office tower suspended above a church; the second joins office and home in an interlocking double spiral that fits precisely within the frame of the office building; and the third is an elaborate pseudo-ecosystem in which waste from the building accumulates around the base of the crane.

This vast structure is an unlikely hybrid of two parallel worlds. Busy city office workers can easily move between the two; their two worlds combine into one, with hard work on the lower level, and relaxation on the upper. Each desk space on the office floors has a fast route to home upstairs; with a nod to No-Stop City, the domestic floor makes the most of a fully serviced environment by locating bathrooms and kitchens in cabins. Unlike Branzi's landscapes, this narrative builds on actual urban context.

In his elaborate 2009 graduation project, again at the Royal College of

Tomas Klassnik, *Desktopolis*, Royal College of Art graduation project, 2006: installation.

Klassnik as a cut-out in his own graduation installation. This cramped workspace contains all he needs to work; he is surrounded by drawings of his latest design, together with a busy in-tray and a ladder to his imaginary living quarters.

Tomas Klassnik, Overview of *Desktopolis*.

Wasted building volume above the churches could radically increase premium office space in the City of London. Poised above Saint Botolph's church, Aldgate, this tower is home to an idealistic narrative combining high-level investment and elaborate recycling.

Art, Tom Greenhall uses narrative twist at every level. *Cultivating Faith* interprets the socio-political context of the time that combined an impending population explosion, with multiculturalism with an Islamic slant. Greenhall's key idea was to re-inhabit a contaminated artificial mountain known affectionately as the Beckton Alps, a landmark on the A13 as it heads east out of London from Whitechapel and Canary Wharf. More or less centred on the peak, and visible for miles up and down the road, sits a sculpted lattice roof in the shape of a cow's head. This auspicious form houses a mosque and, adjacent to it, a series of laboratories for the cultivation of artificial halal meat – in his analysis, a fundamental commodity in short supply given the growth of the local Muslim population.

Tomas Klassnik, Interior of *Desktopolis*.

Sandwiched between each other, work and home occupy interlocking spirals. With echoes of Archizoom's 1969 *No-Stop City*, both work and domestic levels extend as open floors based on Bürolandschaft principles.

Cultivating Faith attempts a leap of understanding; its local planetary system brings out one particular socio-cultural orbit in its architecture, corralling a series of diverse functions into one biotopic narrative. Many of the components, including the model of the cow, were 'found' on the internet, and distorted to suit the design process. Here Greenhall pushes the narrative towards its limits while assembling the 'detritus' that commonly surrounds us.

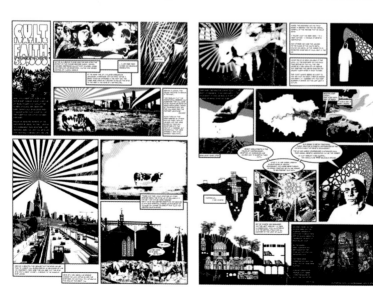

Tom Greenhall, *Cultivating Faith*, Royal College of Art graduation project, 2009: cartoon strip.

With multiculturalism pushed to extreme limits, Greenhall is intrigued by a total socio-environmental system that brings worship and food production into the broad context of the city. The language of cartoons perfectly suits communicating a movie-like scenario beyond the reach of most architects.

Tom Greenhall, Interior of *Cultivating Faith*.

Occupying Beckton Alps, a controversial contaminated site along the A13, this parametric structure based on a cow's head houses a mosque, and next to it, an artificial halal meat production facility.

The use of the human body as a reference point in architecture is not new, dating back to classical rules of proportion, but Tobias Klein (b 1979) has taken it a step further. Klein is not shy about his body – it is his greatest architectural resource and a potential binary double for several projects with a disquieting sense of space. Using MRI scans to help identify solid and space within the human frame, he has researched the interior of

Tobias Klein, *Soft Immortality*, 2008.

The inaccessibility of our own body makes it a legitimate territory for spatial exploration. This technical reconstruction of the central cavity in the chest draws a direct parallel with the voluminous architectural structures intended to instigate a sense of transcendence.

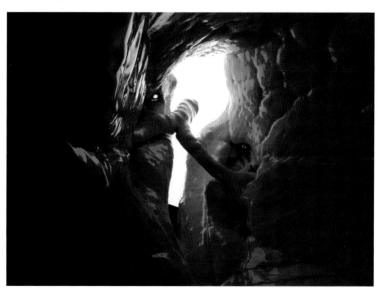

the body extensively, and how it might be recontextualised in architectural vertigo. Many of his images take the viewer inside his body to spaces such as the one between the lungs that is normally occupied by the heart.

Inspired by the excesses of Spanish religious imagery, the *Contoured Embodiment* project (2009) sets out to illustrate a crossover between the Baroque vocabulary and the virtuoso possibilities of digitally augmented architecture. Klein draws data collected from these scans into the reference frame of one of Britain's most classical and iconic buildings, Saint Paul's

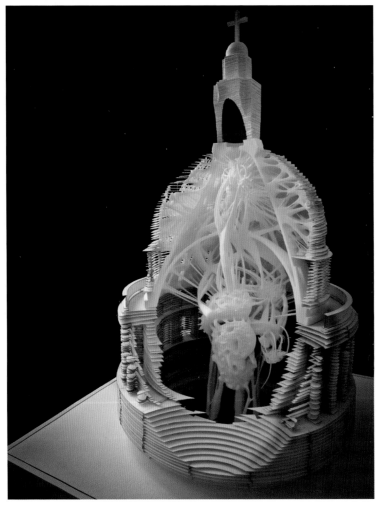

Tobias Klein and Ben Cowd, *Contoured Embodiment*, 2009: model.

In a crossover of architectural bodies, Klein subjects both the dome of Saint Paul's Cathedral and his own heart to MRI scanning techniques. Ignoring differences of scale, he docks the two together to make a complex environment charged with existential significance.

Cathedral (Christopher Wren, 1675–1710). A digitally reconstructed version of his heart to coincide with the central domed space of the cathedral which he has sliced as if it were a body under anatomical investigation. The section reveals a tangible interest in the organic nature of the original dome, and its three constituent parts: an inner cone, and a double dome above and below it.

Although this is very much a project of mind over matter, Klein goes to great lengths to elaborate the ideas three-dimensionally. Like a giant chandelier caught in a web of supporting cables – the connective tissue – the heart hangs in the centre of the space as the ultimate architectural sacrament. Detailed computer-printed maquettes compensate for the abstraction of these manoeuvres, and build them three-dimensionally in our minds. His work captures an existential narrative. 'I am architecture', so to speak.

Narrative rematerialised

In a volte-face of the normal constructive process of design, Kobas Laksa (b 1971) has looked forward in order to look back. The wonderfully crafted images exhibited as 'The Afterlife of Buildings' in the Polish Pavilion at the 11th Venice Architecture Biennale (2008) expose the balance between permanence and impermanence of architecture. Based

Kobas Laksa, *The Metropolitan Prison/2082*, 'The Afterlife of Buildings', Polish Pavilion, 11th Venice Architecture Biennale, Venice, Italy, 2008.

The Metropolitan office building in Warsaw by Norman Foster has become, in Laksa's vision, submerged under a tangle of industrial servicing and heavy-duty urban infrastructure. Like *Blade Runner*, he tells the story of architecture's decay as well as its construction.

Kobas Laksa,
*Sanctuary Lichenian
Waterpark/2032*, 'The
Afterlife of Buildings',
Polish Pavilion, 11th
Venice Architecture
Biennale, Venice, Italy,
2008.

Here the recently completed
Sanctuary of our Lady of
Sorrows, Poland's largest
church, has been subjected
to Laksa's photomontage
skills, and converted into a
water leisure centre.

on six buildings by internationally acclaimed architects built in recent years in Poland, the series postulates how these buildings might look as a result of the unpredictable ravages of time, swings in the economy, and the pressures of the property market.

Once-glittering office buildings by signature names have apparently fallen on hard times, challenging any claim for their durability. In the manner of *Blade Runner*, Laksa distances himself from the normally fetishised perfection of the architectural vision, and is keen to emphasise the fact that buildings are adapted, reshaped, and subject to all kinds of remedial additions, much like the buildings of ancient Rome. He portrays these buildings as vulnerable and subject to unpredictable change once they are free from the architect's control.

Henceforth, says their author, it is the human impact and the passage of time that constitute architecture. Touching a narrative nerve, they emphasise the cumulative effect of change, and how architectural character is as much the result of what the architect had intended. Laksa reinforces the fact that the city is itself a biotopic condition; and life has a way of showing through the thinly veiled perfection of the building. The true architecture of a city arises from the combination of its many parts, and from the balance between order and disorder, certainty and spontaneity, the monumental and the ephemeral.

If you pass the same empty lot every day, sooner or later an idea for its transformation springs to mind. Developers aside, architects are also good at seeing an opportunity. A group of ambitious young architecture students (who came to be known as Assemble) were working at various

Assemble, The Cineroleum, Clerkenwell, London, England, 2010: curtain up.

This enterprising yet equally alternative design converts a defunct petrol filling station into a temporary cinema with witty references to the classic movie house. The original canopy served to cover the ramped seating and support four reflective curtains that would be lowered at the beginning of the performance.

offices including Muf, a London all-woman art and architecture collective,
when they had the idea of turning a disused petrol filling station in
Clerkenwell into a cinema. All that was needed was raked seating, a screen
and a way of enclosing the canopy that stood over the pumps. By the
simplest yet wittiest of means, they turned this vision into reality, in the
form of The Cineroleum (2010).

They would build this cinema themselves from materials begged or
borrowed. An oversized drawstring metallic curtain adorned each side of the
canopy, so that once the audience was seated and the movie about to begin,
these curtains slowly lowered as the titles rolled. Even the retro phenomenon
of cinema delivers romanticism and pragmatics in equal parts, a double which
was perfectly matched by the recast gas station. Narrative follow-through
extended beyond the final result to paper tickets and popcorn. It would be
the place to 'fill up' on the experience of cinema. Even though cars were
more of a memory, The Cineroleum had a whiff of the American drive-in.
With screenings from sundown four nights a week, it hosted offbeat cinema
classics, from *Barbarella* (1968) to *American Gigolo* (1980), *Blade Runner*
(1982) to *Rear Window* (1954).

Full circle

We live in an age of blurred boundaries. The distinction between
architecture, art, and urban and cultural theory grows ever more fluid. It is
clear from the avant-garde work described in this chapter that architects
are no longer the sole protagonists in the creation of the built environment,

or of what is perceived as 'architecture'. But architects still have a crucial role to play. Instead of imposing modes of behaviour on the occupants of the structures and spaces they create, they are called upon to engage with fluctuating conditions and new ways of realising architecture. They should consider an adaptive, layered approach that encompasses the configuration of virtual spaces.

References

1 Ezra Pound, 'Patria Mia', *The New Age* (London), 18 September 1912.
2 James Joyce, *Ulysses*, Shakespeare & Co (Paris), 1922.
3 Rem Koolhaas, *Delirious New York*, Thames & Hudson (London), 1978.
4 Colin Rowe and Fred Koetter, *Collage City*, MIT Press (Cambridge, MA; London), 1978.
5 Voltaire, 'Le Mondain', 1736.
6 Rem Koolhaas, *Delirious New York*, op cit.
7 Aaron Betsky (curator) commenting on 'At Home in the Modern World', Corderie dell'Arsenale, 11th Venice Architecture Biennale, 2008 (quoted widely in press).
8 Ibid.
9 John Maybury and Bernard Tschumi, 'Double Take', Royal College of Art, 2 February 2008.
10 Merlin Coverley, *Psychogeography*, Pocket Essentials (Harpenden), 2007, pp 116–17.
11 Aaron Betsky, *Queer Space: Architecture and Same Sex Desire*, William Morrow (New York), 1997, p 18.

12 Camille Paglia, 'What's Sex Got To Do With It?', *The Sunday Times Magazine*, 12 September 2010.
13 See: Jean Baudrilland, *Simulacra and Simulation*, Sheila Faria Glaser (transl), University of Michigan Press (Ann Arbor), 1994.
14 'La ragione di questa incapacità, direi quasi pudore, nello "spiegare" la propria opera risiede nella natura stessa dell'arte. Infatti solo quando l'opera non è altrimenti spiegabile che attraverso se stessa, possiamo affermare di trovarci di fronte all'arte. È questa ineffabilità il marchio dell'opera autentica.' Carlo Mollino, *Architettura di Parole: Scritti 1933–1965*, Bollati Boringhieri (Turin), 2007, p 389 (author's translation).
15 DBC Pierre in interview with Sean O'Hagan, *The Observer*, 22 August 2010.
16 Author's interview with Gianni Pettena on the Frecciargento train from Florence to Venice, 26 August 2010.
17 See: Ugo La Pietra, *Abitare la Città: ricerche,*

interventi, progetti nello spazio urbano dal 1962 al 1982, Alinea (Florence), 1983. A related exhibition, 'Abitare la Città', was launched at the Fondazione Mudima, Milan in 2008 and subsequently shown at the Fonds Régional d'Art Contemporain, Orléans in 2009.
18 See: Akira Yamaguchi and Yuji Yamashita, *The Art of Akira Yamaguchi*, University of Tokyo Press (Tokyo), 2004.
19 Studio Andrea Branzi, *Per una Nuova Carta di Atene*, first presented at the 4th Urbania festival, Bologna, 2009; also presented at the 12th Venice Architecture Biennale, 2010, and included in its catalogue, pp 100–1.
20 Ibid.
21 Ibid.
22 Marshall McLuhan, *The Gutenberg Galaxy: The Making of Typographic Man*, Routledge & Kegan Paul (London), 1962.
23 Studio Andrea Branzi, op cit.
24 The Klassnik Corporation website, http://www.klassnik.com/pages/exhibitions/Desktopolis.html (accessed 27 March 2011).

Epilogue

In confident economic times everyone seems to know how to build. In rapidly developing parts of the world, say China and Brazil, few questions are asked about how to build a sense of place into a completely new city. Most will imitate their neighbours, and treat new buildings as commodities. The hardest thing is to build a soul into a building. Very few have managed that.

Instant urbanism may once have seemed attractive. When Archigram shot to international attention in the 1960s, their instant cities coincided with and reflected Pop Art. Ten years later, Bernard Tschumi began to reconnect architecture with more philosophical thinking. By the 1980s, narrative emerged as a way of enriching the world we lived in, of animating architecture and cutting the restraints that had prevented it from interacting with the wider world. Now narrative has another role: it provides a method of linking phenomena so as to make sense out of the plethora of conflicting messages and options available to designers today.

Like any other approach to design, narrative architecture has highs and lows. It is not so much a formula for success as a philosophy of design. It raises questions about the language and ethos of the architectural practice, and the integrity and authenticity of what actually gets built. These are difficult times for the profession, which seems to be under siege from all quarters. Much of what was the architectural industry has slowly been transformed into project management, with the architect's leading role in the building process being consigned to the past.

However, the education and culture of architecture have a habit of mutating in such a way that they pop up again where you least expect them. Indeed, there are many people who are not architects, but who would seem, through their movies, artworks and writing, to understand the nature of architecture better than those within the profession. One thinks of authors like Jan Morris (b 1926), Italo Calvino (1923–85), Orhan Pamuk (b 1952) and JG Ballard (1930–2009), none of whom was an architect yet all of whose architectural insight often exceeds that of architects themselves.[1]

Throughout this short exploration of the subject, I have chosen examples that together can help build an understanding. It is of necessity not so much an exploration of categories or rules as a kaleidoscope that assembles luminous fragments into one transformative whole. Yet in all the talk of excess, and letting the experiential rope out, I should stress the fact that restraint is a quality that must be present, regardless of the extent to which a work may be oriented towards the imagination. However diverse the sources, harmony and composition are as important in narrative as they are in any architecture. The same goes for how visual references not only accumulate or disappear, but shift and transform through the design process.

If any reference sticks at a mere reproduction of the original, it is likely to fail. For an appropriate warning you need go no further than Dubai or Las Vegas. In both of these resorts authenticity may be a particularly cherished value, but where the setting ensures everything to be false, the knowingness of the narrative is lost – apparently on the designer as well as on the visitor. Narrative is a stance, and no more believed to be true than the half-timbering on a suburban semi. The Venetian Casino in Las Vegas makes the mistake of trying to be too real. Like Disneyland, it is all pervasive and all prescribed. Little room is left for interpretation. The adjacent 20-storey hotel block might just be a giveaway.

The same is true for many of the even more opulent hotels in Dubai, including the Burj Al Arab and the Madinat Jumeirah, the design of which, according to the promotional material, pays tribute to the ancient Arabian citadel. There is no irony in the way this ancient prototype has been interpreted; the citadel has been adopted not so much to provide a narrative but rather as the source of a caricature, as shallow as a sitcom set.

It is hardly surprising, then, that this kind of pseudo-narrative can be found in every shopping mall and departure lounge around the world. During the two decades spanning the Millennium, lowly forms of narrative were applied to take the rough edges off canteens in every setting, from museums to pubs to high-street coffee shops. Starbucks applies the narrative of the comfy hotel lounge. Heathrow has versions of Yates Wine Lodge. A debased form of narrative adorns every hotel lobby restaurant and ready-furnished apartment reaching out to experience-hungry consumers. We live in a morass of meaningless quotation that is too consistent.

If on the contrary we expect more from architecture, narrative can provide a set of goals that go beyond imitation and style. As we have seen there are many ways in which this narrative layer can be added to the mix, and balance the context/use/narrative triumvirate. To summarise, narrative architecture needs to incorporate a number of the following characteristics:

- Imposed abstract systems such as the musical score or choreographic notation (see Parc de La Villette, Paris, page 45).

- Quotes from the city as a system of overlaps, misconnections, set pieces and accidents (see SESC Pompéia, São Paulo, page 93).

- The emphatic use of spatial language – of enclosure, openness and focus (see The High Line Park, New York, page 95).

- The incorporation of staged non-architectural archetypes that challenge the architectural whole (see Prada Store, New York, page 98).

- Applied geology or naturalistic form that softens the architectural rationale (see Victoria & Albert Museum new entrance and gallery, London, page 98).

- Assemblage of independent functional entities that de-contextualise one another (see BasketBar, Utrecht, page 104).

- Referential layering that heightens attention towards the ludic, the sensual or the spiritual (see Scottish Parliament, Edinburgh, page 105).

- The articulation and distortion of programme that encourages unexpected activity or misuse (see Family House, Isle of Elba, page 108).

- Densely accumulated detail drawn from a coherent 'other' literary or cinematic narrative (see Caffè Bongo, Tokyo, page 113).

- A resonant ready-made construct imported from an exotic time or place (see Jigsaw shop, London, page 115).

- Accelerated decay due to shifting economy or collective desire (see 'The Afterlife of Buildings', Venice, page 153).

- Minor intervention to an existing structure that radically refreshes both purpose and meaning (see The Cineroleum, London, page 155).

Architecture can hardly be narrative unless it contains a degree of tension, and incorporates the visitor in a thinking, being experience. To be narrative, the space, the treatment of surface, the pictures that the building forms around your path all have to engage with you and tease you – to create a field of meaning, without resorting to fake history or atmosphere, that gives off a continuous matrix of time, connects with time, recounts its time, your time, imaginary time. Like a favourite sweater that remembers your body, architecture needs now more than ever to connect through function and with fiction in equal proportions. Narrative is not necessary to keep our heads dry. But if you want that bit extra in a digital age where every form can be achieved, and every world simulated, narrative provides architects with an additional tool drawn from the rich and wonderful world of human nature.

Reference

1 Welsh writer Jan Morris is known for her literary portraits of cities, including Oxford, Venice, Trieste, Hong Kong and New York. Italian author Italo Calvino is best known for his book *Invisible Cities* (first published in Italian as *Le Città Invisibili*, 1972), which comprises prose poems on a series of visionary urban environments. Turkish writer Orhan Pamuk, who initially trained as an architect, came to international recognition with his vivid evocation of Istanbul in *The Black Book*, 1990. English novelist JG Ballard's work is distinguished by a dystopian vision of modernity (see chapter 6).

Bibliography

Emilio Ambasz (ed), *Italy: The New Domestic Landscape*, exhibition catalogue, Museum of Modern Art (New York), 1972.

Iain Borden, Joe Kerr, Alicia Pivaro and Jane Rendell (eds), *Strangely Familiar: Narrative of Architecture in the City*, Routledge (London), 1996.

Marie-Ange Brayer and Frédéric Migayrou (eds), *Archilab: Radical Experiments in Global Architecture*, Thames & Hudson (London), 2003.

Nigel Coates (ed), *NATO* magazine, Issues 1, 2 and 3, Architectural Association (London), 1984–6.

Nigel Coates, *Guide to Ecstacity*, Laurence King (London), 2003.

Francesco Colonna, *Hypnerotomachia Poliphili*, Venice, 1499, first English edition published in London, 1592; contemporary facsimile *Hypnerotomachia Poliphili: The Strife of Love in a Dream*, Benediction Classics (Oxford), 2009.

Joscelyn Godwin, *The Pagan Dream of the Renaissance*, Thames & Hudson (London), 2002.

Zaha Hadid and Patrik Schumaker (eds), *Latent Utopias*, Springer Verlag (Vienna), 2003.

Robert Klanten and Lukas Feireiss (eds), *Beyond Architecture: Imaginative Buildings and Fictional Cities*, Gestalten (Berlin), 2009.

Rem Koolhaas, *Delirious New York: A Retroactive Manifesto for Manhattan*, Thames & Hudson (London), 1978.

Neil Leach (ed), *Rethinking Architecture: A Reader in Cultural Theory*, Routledge (New York, NY; London), 1997.

Kevin Lynch, *The Image of the City*, MIT Press (Cambridge, MA), 1960.

Tom McDonough (ed), *The Situationists and the City*, Verso (London), 2009.

Rick Poynor, *Nigel Coates: The City in Motion*, Fourth Estate (London), 1989.

Colin Rowe and Fred Koetter, *Collage City*, MIT Press (Cambridge, MA; London), 1978.

Iain Sinclair (ed), *London: City of Disappearances*, Hamish Hamilton (London), 2006.

Neil Spiller, *Visionary Architecture: Blueprints of the Modern Imagination*, Thames & Hudson (London), 2006.

John Thackara (ed), *Design after Modernism: Beyond the Object*, Thames & Hudson (London), 1988.

Bernard Tschumi, *The Manhattan Transcripts*, Academy Editions (London), 1981.

Bernard Tschumi and Nigel Coates (eds), *The Discourse of Events*, exhibition catalogue, Architectural Association (London), 1983.

Mark Wigley, *Constant's New Babylon: The Hyper-architecture of Desire*, 010 Uitgeverij (Rotterdam), 1998.

Index

Figures in italics indicate captions.